Inside:

MW00452736

The famous warships

NAVAL ARCHIVES

Vol 9 • First Edition • Lublin 2018

ISBN: 978-83-65437-92-1

Editor-in-chief: Damian Majsak
Assistant editor: Kamil Stopiński
Translation/Proof-reading: T. Basarabowicz
e-mail: redakcja@kagero.pl
phone +4881 501-21-05
DTP: Kagero Studio

Editorial board reserves the right to shorten texts and changing of titles and also is not responsible for author's opinions contained in texts. Non ordered materials will not be returned.

Publisher:
KAGERO Publishing
Akacjowa 100, Turka, os. Borek,
20-258 Lublin 62, Poland
www.kagero.pl, kagero@kagero.pl

Marketing:
Joanna Majsak marketing@kagero.pl

Sales: e-mail: oferta@kagero.pl,
phone/fax +4881 501-21-05

Radetzky-Class
– Forgotten Battleships Of The Forgotten Navy

Witold Koszela

"Erzherzog Franz Ferdinand" in a beautiful view from the starboard side.

These were very interesting ships, one of a kind and successful, but also too late for their time. Lack of more interesting events related to their service, remaining idle at anchor for almost the entire period of World War One and finally the collapse of Austria-Hungary means that nowadays, overshadowed by the much larger, better armed and better-known battleships of the Tegetthoff-class, no one remembers about these ships any longer.

The Navy

Battleships of the Radetzky-class are commonly considered as transitional vessels between the Erzherzog Karl pre-Dreadnought and the first Dreadnoughts in the Austro-Hungarian fleet, ie the Tegetthoff-class, also known as the Viribus Unitis type, and despite their almost non-existent combat service, they can be considered quite successful and contributing a lot to the Navy. Before discussing how they were built, it is worth recalling the difficult and convoluted path that had to be overcome before they were designed.

The prevailing conviction in the second half of the nineteenth century among the senior rep-

resentatives of the dual monarchy was that the existing fleet was sufficient to defend the relatively small eastern coast of the Adriatic, effectively inhibited its development, especially since the Kaiserliche und Königliche Kriegsmarine was not intended for offensive operations, which only meant that matters related to it were often pushed into the background, while the focus was on land forces.

For this reason, the slow development of the fleet, which began after a stagnation lasting more than twenty years, could be observed only when in 1890 Adm. Sterneck took over the post of the Supreme Commander of the Navy.

It was then that the first two large cruisers "Kaiser Franz Joseph I" and "Kaiserin Elisabet" appeared, and soon after them in 1893 another and much more modern vessel the "Kaiserin und Koning Maria Theresia".

In the same year the construction of the most interesting vessels - the first battleships - "Monarch", "Wien" and "Budapest" commenced. These ships, designed by Ing. Siegfried Popper (1848 - 1933) – who was behind all subsequent battleships of the K.u.K. fleet - due to lack of resources

had a displacement of only 5,636 tons and armament consisting of four 240 mm and six 150 mm guns, which meant that they were later classified as coastal defence battleships. The more powerful ships of this type had yet to wait.

It was only in 1902-1904 that the first "larger" battleships entered service: "Habsburg", "Arpad" and "Babenberg" armed with three 240 mm and twelve 150 mm guns. They were very interesting vessels, but still quite small.

Their full displacement amounted to 8,964 tons and they featured very complex, tall casemates in the midship area, which later turned out to be a serious stability problem in spite of their sinister silhouettes. In the meantime, other types of ships were also commissioned.

In 1899-1901, the first modern cruiser, classified as armoured, "Kaiser Karl VI" with a displacement of 7,300 tons entered service, armed with two 240 mm and eight 150 mm guns, and three smaller cruisers "Zenta", "Aspern" and "Szigetvar" with a displacement of 2,500 t and armament consisting of eight 120 mm guns.

Two years later another armoured cruiser "Sankt Georg" entered the line, a semi-sister ship of the aforementioned "Kaiser Karl VI" with a displacement of 8,199 tons and armament consisting of two 240 mm, five 190 mm and four 150 mm guns.

At the same time, shipbuilding work began on the next three battleships named "Erzherzog Karl", "Erzherzog Friedrich" and "Erzherzog Ferdinand Max" with a displacement of 11,780 tons and main armament consisting of four 240 mm and twelve 190 mm guns.

These by far the most powerful ships in the Austro-Hungarian fleet were unusually interesting and undoubtedly designed under the influence of similar constructions previously built in Britain, Italy and France.

However, when in 1906 the prototype "Erzherzog Karl" was commissioned, in distant Great Britain, another ship entered service which completely revolutionized the former concept of a battleship. HMS "Dreadnought", as you can easily guess, meant that in just in one moment the most powerful and most modern battleships of the K.u.K. fleet became obsolete, which could not even be helped by their splendid looking profiles with three funnels, which until recently testified to the "power" of the ship.

Even worse, in mid-1904, preliminary designs of new battleships were being developed and, as it would turn out, they did not have much in common with the revolutionary British project.

Confusion about the "Dreadnought"

When in 1904 in the Marinesektion (Navy Section at the Ministry of War) the first orders were issued to start preliminary design work on new battleships, few of its representatives were aware of the seriousness of the fact that similar projects were underway in Britain, the effect of which was to trigger a real revolution in shipbuilding and to make battleships start dividing into "Dreadnoughts" and less valuable "pre-Dreadnoughts" from the moment when HMS "Dreadnought" entered service.

In fact, the problem was not in the lack of openness to modern solutions or ignorance of what is happening in the shipyards of other fleets.

Simply, such a mighty ship as this battleship, most importantly armed according to the concept of "All big gun" was a vessel much bigger than those built earlier and armed with three or

"Zrinyi" from the port side. A characteristic feature allowing the identification of Radetzky battleships were their cranes, whose arms in the case of "Zrinyi" pointed towards the bow.

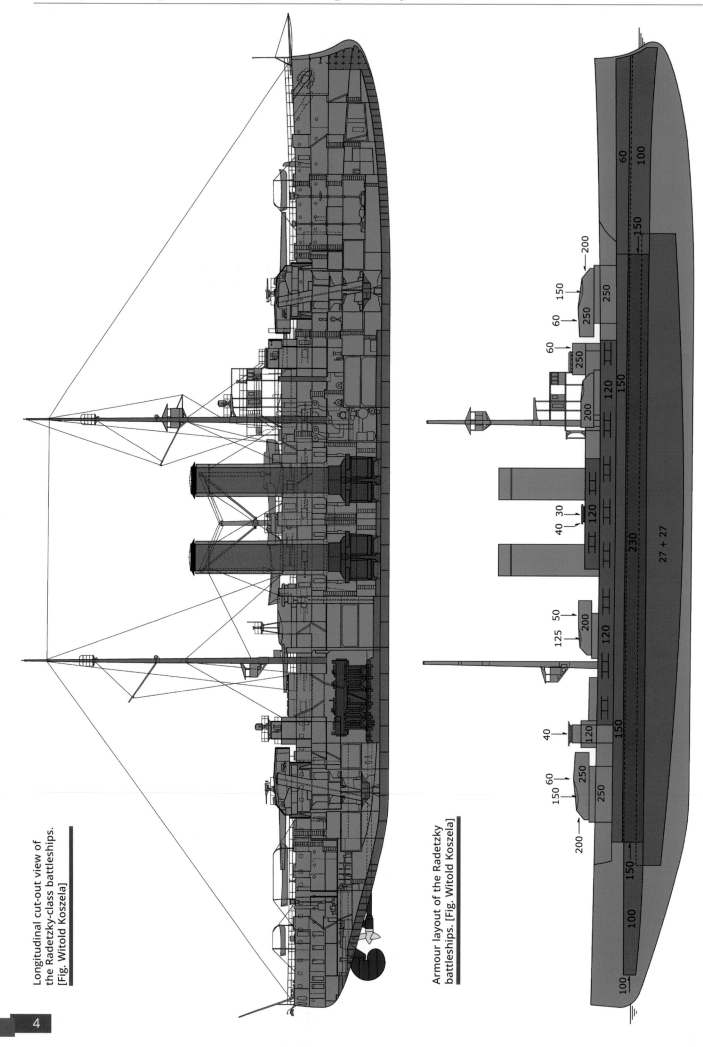

Longitudinal cut-out view of
the Radetzky-class battleships.
[Fig. Witold Koszela]

Armour layout of the Radetzky
battleships. [Fig. Witold Koszela]

four large calibre guns, and the rest of the smaller one, and so she had a much greater displacement, which in the case of "Dreadnought" reached 18,400 tons.

The larger ship, with higher costs, and in the complicated Austro-Hungarian reality, one could not afford it, all the more that it was not only about the cost of construction, but about almost the entire infrastructure.

The fleet did not possess a dock that could accommodate a ship of a size similar to the "Dreadnought", or even a smaller one of approximately 16,000 tons, ie the displacement which was calculated in his assumptions by the aforementioned chief designer Siegfried Popper, and that meant the need to build a new dock and therefore further costs.

Similar problems could be found in the case of the shipyards and armament industry, in this case Škoda, which at that time were just beginning to produce guns of large calibres.

With all these problems, but not yet fully, the K.u.K. Navy managed to deal with the design and construction of the Tegetthoff battleships, but now there could be no question of introducing a "revolution" in such an underfunded force as the fleet.

However, the design work was ongoing, and the state of their advancement changed significantly when the new Supreme Commander, Adm. Rudolf Montecuccoli (1843-1922) introduced in July 1905 his plan to expand the fleet to 12 battleships, 4 armoured cruisers, 8 cruisers, 18 destroyers, 36 torpedo ships and 6 submarines. As you can guess, it could not be achieved without continuing the design work, and by the autumn of 1905 these ended with the development of five preliminary projects designated A, B, C, D and E,

ships of similar displacement and dimensions, but with a highly diversified armament.

The first project marked as A, proposed a battleship armed with four 280 mm placed guns in two two-barrel turrets, located at the bow and stern in the ship's plane of symmetry and four 240mm guns placed in four single-barrel turrets located amidships, two on each side.

This main battery was supposed to be supplemented with eight 190 mm guns placed in hull casemates, below the main deck.

It is easy to see that this project provided for the construction of ships with almost identical layout to the Erzherzog Karl-class with slightly increased firepower in the form of 240 mm guns, so the project did not bring too much new.

The next B project was equipped similarly - four 280 mm guns in two turrets and four 240 mm guns in four individual broadside turrets.

Here, however, the number and the calibre of guns installed in the hull casemates was changed to twelve 100 mm guns.

The third C project was much more interesting and assumed the construction of a ship armed with eight 280 mm placed in four two-barrel turrets, located at the bow and stern, and two on the sides midships.

This was supposed to be supplemented with sixteen 100 mm guns and it is hard not to notice that had this project was implemented, the new Radetzky battleships would be able to become something of the first Austro-Hungarian Dreadnoughts with unified main battery of the same calibre.

Similarly, it would be in the case of D project, which provided for the construction of ships armed with six 305 mm and sixteen 100 mm guns arranged in the same way as in project C, with the

Battleship "Erzherzog Franz Ferdinand" seen from the starboard.

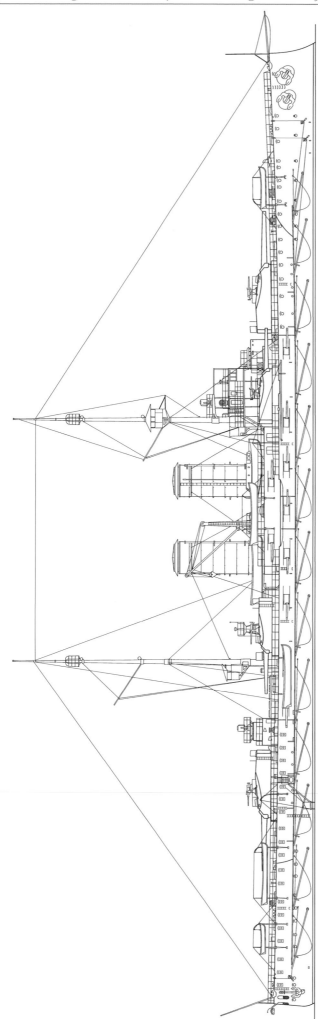

Radetzky-class battleships featured very modest superstructures, which was intended by the designers to limit the target area for enemy gunfire. [Fig. Witold Koszela]

difference that the broadside turrets would be single-barrel ones.

The last project marked as E was the closest to the battleships eventually built and assumed the construction of ships armed with four 305 mm guns in two turrets at the bow and stern, eight 190 mm guns in four turrets and sixteen 100 mm guns arranged in broadside and superstructure casemates. Anyway, a committee assembled later, whose actual task was to be selecting the final project, after long debates, chose this one, recognizing it as the most appropriate for the needs of the fleet, introducing some modifications in the form of changing the 190 mm calibre guns to 240 mm and an increase in the number of 100 mm guns to twenty.

This project was chosen, although it is worth noting that there were objections, such as from Siegfried Popper himself who stood quite firmly in favour of the solutions applied to the Dreadnought-class ships.

The decisions, however, had been made and one had to reconcile with them, recognizing this new type of battleship as something of a transitional construction between the old and the new and classified as semi-Dreadnought.

Radetzky-class semi-Dreadnoughts

Once the final selection had been made, the E project was sent for further design and construction work, and finally building of the ships began.

The order for construction of all three vessels was placed at the private Stabilimento Tecnico Triestino shipyard in San Marco near Trieste, whose two large slipways could accommodate the largest Austro-Hungarian warships.

A part of the work was also commissioned at the Seearsenal in Pola owned by the Navy, which had suitable docks and a 240-ton floating crane.

The keel for the battleship marked as Schlachtschiff-I, later Radetzky, was laid on 26 November 1907, and the launch took place on 3 July 1909.

The second battleship Schlachtschiff-II Hunyadi, whose name was later changed to Zriny, was not launched until 12 April 1910, while the third, Schlachtschiff-III Erzherzog Franz Ferdinand, was launched on 30 September 1908.

At this point, it should be noted that the representative ship of the whole class should be „Erzherzog Franz Ferdinand", whose keel laying, launching and entry into service took place the earliest, but the similarity of the name of the ship to the previously introduced Erzherzog Karl-class battleships, and especially „Ferdinand Max", would have meant that both types could have been constantly confused and at a meeting which took place on 8 March 1909 at the office of the Navy Section presidium, it was decided that the new class of ships would be classified as Radetzky.

The total cost of construction of these ships amounted to 118,219,853 crowns, which far exceeded the state budget adopted for this purpose.

The ships' profile

Battleships of the Radetzky-class featured a compact, flush-decked hull with a total length of 138.7 m, length between perpendiculars 131.1 m, beam 24.5 m and a draft of 8 m.

The main deck continued uninterrupted from the bow to the stern of the ships, which allowed for significant weight savings, but the lack of deck elevation in the bow part caused deterioration of the seaworthiness of the ships. The bow was typical of ships from that era, under the waterline it had the shape of a battering ram then gently passed into a straight keel.

The ships received so-called cruiser sterns, in which a technical novelty was introduced in the form of an aft gallery, consisting of five huge openings equipped with decorative balustrades adjacent to the accommodation of the ship's commander.

On each side of the hull, one keel was placed to reduce the lateral list of the ships.

Battleships of the Radetzky-class were also characterized by very modest superstructures, unprecedented in other fleets, which according to the theories of their constructors was aimed at the maximum reduction of the chance of a hit by the enemy's fire.

The fore superstructure consisted of an armoured command post and placed above it, slightly rearward, the wheelhouse mounted on light openwork structures.

Further amidships there were small single-storey superstructures, ending on the sides of the casemates for 100 mm guns, which were covered with a narrow deck in the shape of a horseshoe, descending towards the bow up to the wheelhouse.

In their central part there were two huge funnels, openwork structures for ship's boats and two cranes for their servicing, and here it is worth paying attention to a certain curiosity, such as cranes whose arms, due to the almost identical-looking silhouettes of ships, were directed in various directions, which was supposed to be the main element of their identification.

And so the arms of the cranes on "Radetzky" were directed towards the stern, on "Zrinyi" in the direction of the bow, and on "Erzherzog Franz Ferdinand" the port side crane towards the bow, while the starboard one towards the stern.

A certain difference affecting the appearance of the ship's silhouettes was also their fairly diversified boat equipment.

Here, in the case of "Radetzky", on the structures around the funnels and boat davits there were: 2 steam longboats, 2 first class longboats, 1 first class rescue cutter, 3 first class cutters, 1 first class gig, 1 third class gig, 2 yawls, 2 jolly boats and 2 working jolly boats.

On "Zrinyi" there were: 1 steam longboat, 2 first class longboats, 2 motor launches, 1 first class rescue cutter, 3 first class cutters, 1 first class gig, 1 third class gig, 2 yawls, 2 jolly boats and 2 working jolly boats.

It was completely different in the case of "Erzherzog Franz Ferdinand" and the equipment consisted of: 1 first class steam longboat, 1 fast first class launch, 1 second class launch, 2 first class longboats, 1 first class rescue cutter, 3 cutters, 2 first class gigs, 1 second class gig, 2 yawls, 2 jolly boats and 2 working jolly boats.

Further to the stern, there were only the engine room skylights, small deck equipment and the aft command post. The entire silhouette was completed by two masts, up to 45 meters in height, with observation posts and antennas.

Another curiosity very characteristic of the appearance of these ships was their painting scheme, because all three vessels in the first years of service were painted almost overall with olive colour - as we know very unusual for warships and unheard of in other fleets.

Why was that so? Well, it had to do with the Commander-In-Chief of the Navy, Admiral Rudolf Montecuccoli, according to whom such a colour was optimal for blending the silhouette against the mountainous and green Adriatic coasts.

Opinions on this subject, however, varied and not everyone agreed with such reasoning, which can be evidenced by the decision made by Admiral Anton Haus already in the first days on his new post as Commander-In-Chief, who ordered replacing this camouflage scheme with a light grey colour.

Armour and anti-torpedo protection

Radetzky battleships' armour did not bring any spectacular revolution to shipbuilding. Their hulls were shielded by an armoured citadel made of Krupp cemented steel (KC-Krupp Cementiert).

"Radetzky" during launching ceremony, 3 July 1909.

Basic specifications of the Radetzky-class ships	
Standard displacement	14,508 t
Full displacement	15,845 t ("Zrinyi" 15,847 t)
Overall length	138.7 m
Waterline length	137.4 m
Length between perpendiculars	131.1 m
Beam	24.5 m
Draft	8.0 m
Propulsion	2 four-cylinder, triple expansion steam engines. 20, 600 HP, 24 Yarrow coal boilers, two propellers
Speed	20.5 kn ("Radetzky" 20.1 kn)
Coal supply	1,854 t
Oil supply	188 t
Range	4,000 nm (at 10 kn)
Ship's company	30 officers, 845–860 NCOs and men
Armour:	
Citadel	230 mm/150 mm/100 mm
Casemates	120 mm
Decks	30 mm +18 mm, slopes 36 mm
Command posts	250 mm/60 mm
305 mm gun turrets	250 mm/ 150–200 mm/60 mm
240 mm gun turrets	200 mm/ 150–125 mm/50 mm
Armament	4 × 305 mm L/45 Škoda 8 × 240 mm L/45 Škoda 20 × 100 mm L/50 Škoda 6 × 66 mm L/45 Škoda 2 × 47 mm L/33 Hotchkiss 4 × 47 mm L/44 Škoda 4 × 8 mm M 7/12 Schwarzlose machine guns 4 × 450 mm torpedo tubes

Its belt, which was over three meters high, had a thickness of 230 mm in the area of the midships and main battery turrets, and in the region of the bow and stern it was 100 mm thick.

In addition, under the armour there was a 50mm teak backing, which, combined with an 18 mm thick plate sheet, would provide additional protection and absorb the effects of a possible explosion.

Teak primer is clearly seen in the photos of launching the ships, which may allow us to get acquainted with the distribution of the described protection.

The aforementioned citadel ended just behind the barbettes and was closed with transverse bulkheads 150 mm thick, and just over the 230-mm belt ran the same with a thickness of 150 mm.

Inside, outside the outline of the citadel, 1.8 m away from the sides of the citadel, 54 mm thick antitorpedo bulkheads were placed, while the casemates of the broadsides, as well as the superstructures for the 100 mm guns, were covered with 120 mm thick armour.

The armoured deck consisted of two 30 mm and 18 mm thick plates.

The slopes of the armoured deck stretched laterally to the lower edge of the armoured belt and were 36 mm thick.

The whole hull armour was complemented by a system commonly used in those days of antitorpedo nets, consisting of 24 nets (12 per side) with dimensions 7 × 9 m manufactured by a British company called Bullivant. These nets were laid out on 26 special fittings stretched by means of a complicated system of ropes and blocks.

This protection did not fully meet the expectations set for it, so during the war, similarly as on ships in other fleets, these nets - unusually troublesome to fold and unfold - were dismantled. Returning to the description of the armour, the main command post had 250 mm thick walls and a 60 mm thick roof. Stern and broadside posts received walls from 120 mm to 100 mm thick and roofs from 40 mm to 30 mm.

The main battery turrets were shielded with armour - sides 250 mm, walls inclined from 150 mm to 200 mm, roofs 60 mm and barbettes 250 mm.

Turrets of the 240 mm guns were shielded with 200 mm armour on the sides, walls inclined from 150 mm to 125 mm, roofs 50 mm.

Propulsion system

Similarly to the armour of the described battleships, this was not a novelty considering the fact that in such breakthrough constructions as Dreadnought, apart from unified weapons, the norm was steam turbines allowing ships to develop much higher speeds than in the case of traditional steam engines.

In the case of the Radetzky vessels, this solution was not chosen and they were equipped with twelve „traditional" Yarrow coal boilers with 24 burners and additional oil fuel burners installed.

These boilers powered with steam two vertical, four-cylinder triple expansion piston engines, which drove two three-bladed propellers with a diameter of 5,250 mm.

The propulsion systems on individual ships reached 20,288 HP for "Erzherzog Franz Ferdinand", which allowed for sailing at 20.58 knots, 19,437 HP for "Radetzky", which allowed it to reach speeds of 20.16 knots and 19,860 HP for "Zrinyi", which gave a speed of 20.50 knots.

Additionally, steam generators for generating electricity with a voltage of 100V were installed on the vessels.

The above-mentioned 12 coal-fired boilers required enormous fuel supplies, which is why on Radetzky-class battleships coal bunkers were provided that could accommodate from 1,298 to 1,854 tons of coal.

In addition, there were tanks for 188 tons of oil on the ships, which together allowed for 4,000 nm of sailing at a speed of 10 knots, however, some sources give ranges at 5,000 nm or even 5,600 nm? How it was actually, we would most likely never find out...

Armament

Armament of Radetzky-class battleships consisted of four 305 mm L/41 calibre guns, eight 240 mm L/45 guns, twenty 100 mm L/50 guns, six 66 mm L/45 guns and three 450 mm torpedo tubes.

These were supplemented by Hotchkiss cal. 44 mm L/33 quick-firing cannons, Škoda cal. 47 mm

Simplified outlines of basic projects that were taken into account in the construction of Radetzky-class battleships. [Fig. Witold Koszela]

PROJEKT „A"

PROJEKT „B"

PROJEKT „C"

PROJEKT „D"

PROJEKT „E"

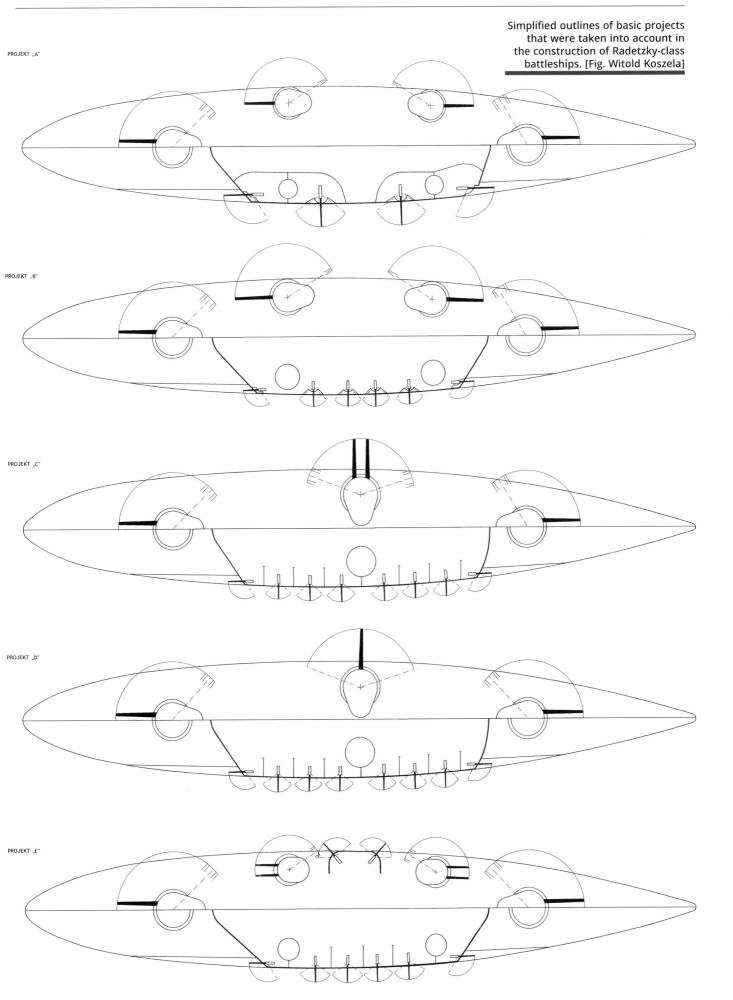

L/44 anti-aircraft guns and Schwarzlose M 7/12 machine guns.

The main battery consisted of four 305 mm L/45 guns mounted in two double-barrel turrets arranged at the bow and stern in the ship's plane of symmetry.

Both the guns themselves and their turrets were provided by Škoda-Werke A.G. from Pilsen, which at that time began to gain more and more experience in the production of this type of gun and became the main supplier of weapons for ships of the Austro-Hungarian fleet.

One 305 mm L/45 cannon together with breech weighed 54.6 tons and they were placed in two, half-round armoured turrets powered by electric motors, to which ammunition was fed by special feeders from magazines below the waterline.

The cannons mounted in the turrets had an elevation from -4 ° to + 20 °, but a shell could only be loaded at an angle of + 2.5 °. The rate of fire, depending on the angle of elevation, was 1.5 to 2 rounds per minute, and the range reached 17,750 metres at 19° angle of elevation. The supply of ammunition amounted to 150 armour piercing and 150 high explosive rounds.

It is worth noting that the turrets had a novel technical solution in the form of mounting both on their roofs and the roofs of the 24-cm turrets the 66 mm L/45 guns, which could be coupled with the large-calibre barrels and fire instead of them. Of course, this solution was developed for gunnery training, during which in this way the crews could gain experience without consuming expensive large calibre shells.

The supplementary main battery – indirect, consisted of eight 240 mm L/45 guns. They were arranged in the same way as the 305 mm gun in four double barrel turrets, which were placed two on each side amidships. The turrets themselves were almost identical to those of the 305 mm guns, being only slightly smaller and less heavily armoured. These guns and turrets were also produced and delivered by Škoda's plants. A single gun with breech weighed 27.7 tons, fired 215 kg armour piercing shells and 103 kg HE rounds, while the weight of the propellant charge reached 70 kg.

Similarly to the 305 mm calibre guns, their elevation angle was between -4 ° and + 20 °, the rate of fire was 1.5 to 2.5 shots/min, and the range at 12° was 12,000 m, while at 8° it fell to 10,000 m.

The supply of ammunition amounted to 160 armour piercing and 640 HE rounds.

The medium guns were placed in the hull casemates and at the sides of the superstructure, and there were twenty 100 mm L/50 guns. This was a very modern weapon, constructed also at the Škoda factory. The weight of a single gun with breech was 7.7 tons, and the projectile was 13.7 kg. They were set on special rocking mounts inside the armoured casemates, which significantly affected their limited angles of barrel elevation.

The elevation angle in the vertical plane was -6 ° to + 15 °, while in the horizontal plane from 120° to 140° depending on the casemate in which they were placed. Their theoretical rate of fire was 20 to 25 shots per minute, while the ammunition stock amounted to 6,000 rounds.

Light guns were represented by six single 66 mm L/45 guns, which were placed individually on the tops of the main battery turrets[1]. During the war, newer 66 mm L/50 Model 1910 guns were characterized by slightly larger elevation and range.

Light guns also include two Hotchkiss quick-firing guns 47 mm L/33, four Škoda 47 mm L/44 anti-aircraft guns and four Schwarzlose M 7/12 machine guns, which were mounted depending on the needs on board or on the ships' boats.

In addition to artillery equipment, the ships were equipped with three 450 mm torpedo tubes, which were placed under the waterline, one on the bow and two on the sides approximately at the level of the main command post.

The bow tube was positioned exactly along the axis of the hull symmetry, while the broadside tubes were positioned at an angle of 63° towards the bow.

The weight of a single torpedo was 630 kg, and their stock amounted ten units. In addition, twenty C/08 mines were taken aboard, which, depending on the need, could be laid by the ships' longboats.

Finally, a few words should be mentioned about fire control systems, which in the case of Radetzky ships were extremely poor and consisted of two rangefinders from Barr & Stroud with an optical base of 2.73 m placed on the sides midships, used to control fire the of the 10 cm guns.

During service, on the roof of the main command post a small rangefinder appeared with a base of 1.37 m for firing the 66 mm guns, while on the roof of the stern command post a 3 m type Zeiss rangefinder was placed, which after 1916 was replaced with a rangefinder of 5 m base, also Zeiss type.

Endnotes

[1] Their official name was 7 cm L/45 TAG K 09 gun.

Radetzky in the full gala, August 1911.

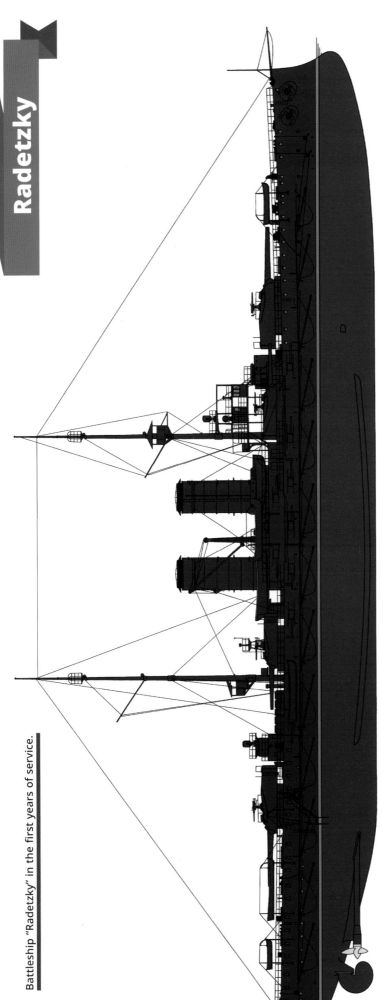

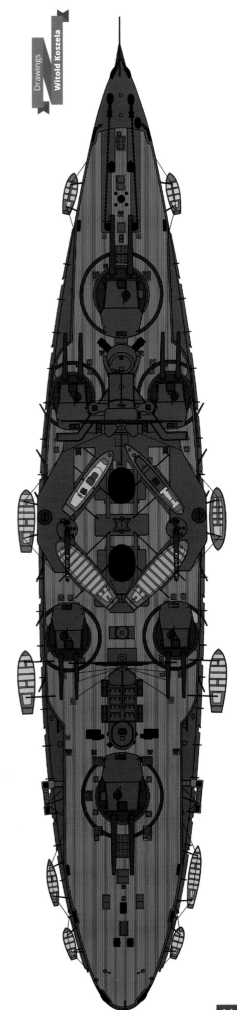

Battleship

Radetzky

Battleship "Radetzky" in the first years of service.

Drawings
Witold Koszela

The Polish Destroyer

ORP GROM

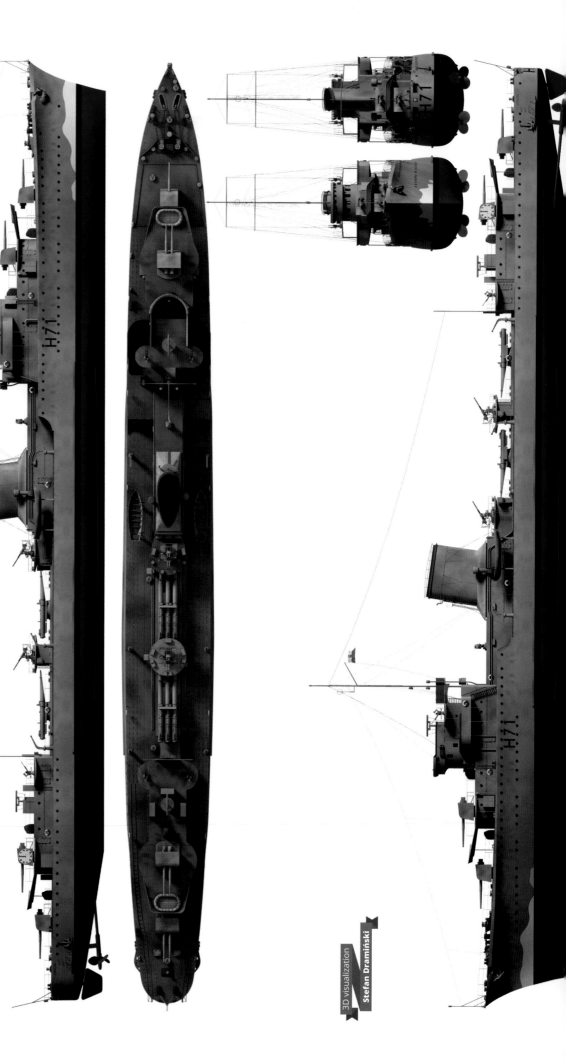

3D visualization
Stefan Dramiński

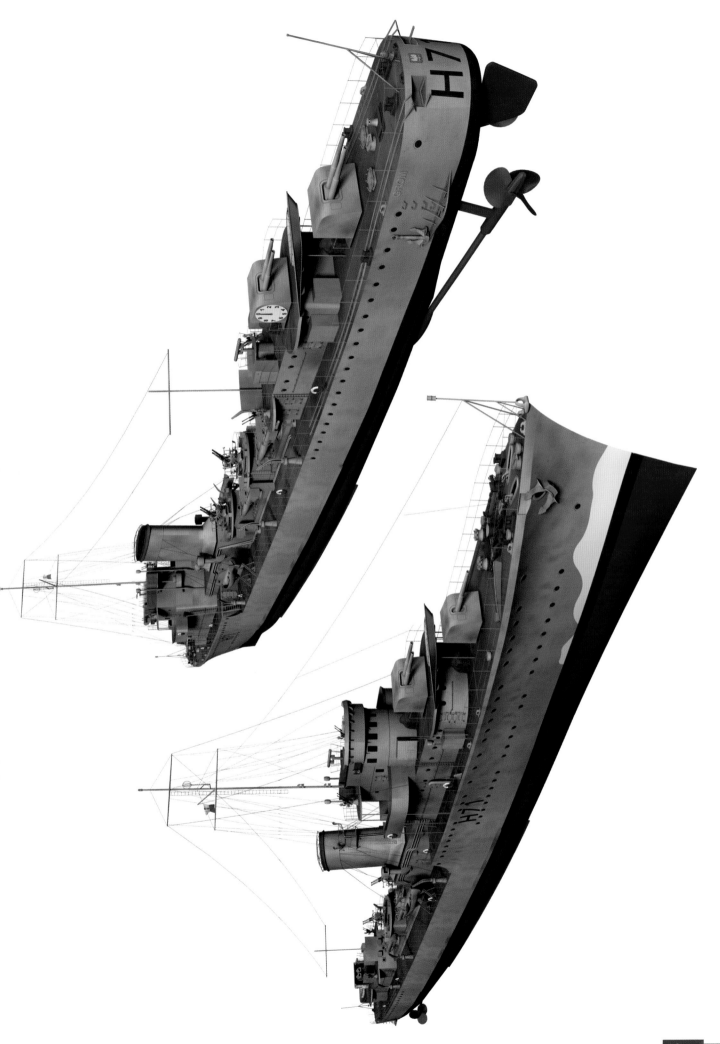

Three Embodiments Of The "Seydlitz"

Jan Radziemski

"Seydlitz" during the fitting out works - the end of 1939. A funnel is visible, the bow already has an Atlantic stem. In the background, you can see the destroyer Z 23.

The story of the German cruiser "Seydlitz" is full of many interesting threads and unexpected twists. Designed as the light cruiser "K", she was launched as the heavy cruiser "Seydlitz" and ended her career as an aircraft carrier (which was in uncompleted state though). When she was almost ready, she was disassembled almost to a half. During her short life, she changed from the German banner to the Soviet flag, at least once she burned and sank twice, each time thanks to her current owners. And it all happened to her in just one decade.

The treaty dilemmas

The restrictive provisions of the Treaty of Versailles did not allow Germany to freely develop her fleet. In the first half of the 1930s, six light cruisers were built there with displacement limited to 6,000 tons and 150 mm main guns. At that time, other naval powers were building larger, more heavily armed and better armoured ships of this type. Moreover, as a result of the resolutions of the Washington conference, in 1922 a race of naval powers in the category of heavy cruisers began, the so-called Washington cruisers (displacement up to 10,000 tons and armament up to 8 inches, ie 203 mm). The Germans did not feel like staying out of the way and watching other fleets grow in strength. The Reichsmarine's supreme command faced the problem of choosing the right type of cruiser that best suited Germany's maritime doctrine, and on the other hand fulfilling the conditions of naval agreements regarding this type of ship. To a large extent, this dilemma was solved in 1933 with Hitler coming to power. From that moment on, the Germans ceased to care about the treaty restrictions, although they had quietly broken them earlier. On 16 March 1935, Hitler unilaterally renounced the Treaty of Versailles, but as part of the tactics of putting his opponents at ease, on 18 June 1935 he signed a maritime agreement in London between Britain and Germany. The agreement determined the ratio of German-British naval forces, which was to be 35:100, with the exception of submarines. Thanks to this, the Kriegsmarine could build five heavy cruisers with a total displacement of 51,380 tons.

The first two cruisers were ordered before the events described above[1]. Taking into consideration the displacement of 10,000 tons fixed for this category of ships, it gave the opportunity to build (next to the two already ordered) an additional three more vessels of this class. The impediment, as it later would turn out to be irrelevant, was the clause included under the pressure of the British side, according to which the last two cruisers should be armed with 150 mm guns. However, the Germans were left with a "gate" in the form of a provision of the right to complete them with 203-mm guns in the case that "special circumstances" would occur, eg a threat from another country. For this reason, in November 1935, only one cruiser was ordered. In the case of the other two, it was decided to wait for the appropriate moment when "special circumstances" arose. In the meantime, further restrictions appeared instead. The second London Maritime Conference, which took place from 9 December 1935 to 25 March 1936, introduced a de facto ban on the construction of new heavy cruisers. Although Germany was not a participant in the conference, and its findings were not binding, Hitler wanted to show that he was in accord with the opinion of the Western powers, although as usual it was only a subterfuge. In these circumstances, the construction of the last two cruisers with 150 mm guns was officially announced.

Light, heavy or light-heavy cruiser?

The heavy cruisers, later called the Admiral Hipper class, began to be designed in 1934 under the direction of Dr. G. Burchardt. Initially, they were defined by successive letters of the alphabet (G, H, J). Keels for these ships were laid in 1935-1936. On 8 June 1936, Admiral E. Raeder decided to order two more cruisers designated with the letters K and L. Unlike their predecessors, they were to be armed with 150 mm guns (149.1 mm), but the order was changed on 18 September. In addition to the variant with 150 mm guns, a variant with 203 mm calibre armament was to be created. It was a clever ploy, because barbettes for turrets with 150 mm guns did not differ from barbettes for 203 mm guns. In all other elements, the project repeated its predecessors' solutions. The main

differences were only in armament and propulsion. The cruisers K and L were to receive twelve SKL/55 C/28 150 mm guns, placed in four, three barrelled C/34 turrets, two at the bow and two at the stern.

The supplementary battery was to consist of twelve 105 mm Flak L/65 C 33 guns on six twin barrelled stabilized C/37 mounts. Anti-aircraft battery consisted of twelve 37 mm Flak L/83 C/30 guns on twin barrelled C/30 mounts. Its complement was to be eight 20 mm FlaMG L/65 C/30 quick-firing guns on single C/30 mounts. The ships were to receive strong torpedo equipment in the form of twelve 533 mm calibre tubes for G7 torpedoes.

Two pneumatic catapults and one 22 metre hangar were the aircraft equipment. Three floatplanes were to be based on the ships: two with folded wings in a hangar and one placed on a catapult. Both catapults rotated 360 degrees.

The M 1935 system was used to control the main battery fire, analogous to that installed on battleships of the Gneisenau class. It included three rangefinders: two with a base of seven me-

The hull of "Seydlitz" slowly slides off the slipway at the shipyard.

Tab. 1. Specifications of the "Seydlitz" heavy cruiser	
Parameter	
Displacement, t	
standard	14,240
normal (construction)	17,600
full	19,800
Dimensions, m	
length overall/waterline (after modernisation)	207.70/199.50 (212.50)
beam	21.90/20.00
draft, displacement normal/full	6.57/7.94
Height, m	12.45
Propulsion	
Number of turbines × output, HP	3 × 44,000
Mx. speed, knots.	32
Fuel supply: normal/max., t	1798/3271.2
Crew	1409

Tab. 2. "Seydlitz" construction chronology	
18.07.1936	Order for the "K" type cruiser
29.12.1936	Keel laid at the Deschimag yard in Bremen
19.01.1939	Launching ceremony of the "Seydlitz"
26.08.1942	Start of conversion into aircraft carrier (Project "Weser-1")
01.01.1943	Work on the "Seydlitz" suspended
30.03.1943	"Seydlitz" towed from Bremen to Konigsberg
02.04.1943	"Seydlitz" arrives in Konigsberg
29.01.1945	"Seydlitz" scuttled in Konigsberg
10.04.1945	The wreck of "Seydlitz" seized by the Soviets
25.05.1945	"Seydlitz" raised from the bottom by the EPRON detachment
10.03.1947	"Seydlitz" listed as a Soviet Navy ship
09.04.1947	"Seydlitz" removed from the Soviet Navy listing
24.08.1947	"Seydlitz" scuttled in the waters of the Gulf of Finland

tres and one of six metres. None of the four main gun turrets had its own rangefinder. The supplementary battery fire was controlled from four SL-8 posts with four metre rangefinders.

The K cruiser had the same hull and armour as the other ships of the series (in July 1939 she received an elongated Atlantic stem). It differed from the previous three vessels in terms of the drive equipment used, although the number of turbines (three) and their output remained the same. For the first time, Wagner-Deschimag turbines were used on large Kriegsmarine warships. It was a completely new construction. Each turbine set achieved 44,000 hp at 320 rpm. The economic output of the turbines was 10,500 hp at 118 rpm. The turbines were placed in two compartments separated by a room accommodating the auxiliary machinery. The assembly of the central shaft was placed in compartment III, and the devices driving the outer shafts were placed in compartment V. Unlike the predecessors, the K cruiser had only nine boilers, instead of twelve. They were located in three boiler rooms in compartments VI, VII and VIII. Wagner type boilers with forced circulation produced steam with a working pressure of 59 atm and a temperature of 450° C. The boiler's capacity was 56 t/h. The ship had three propellers with a diameter of 4.10 m and one rudder. Electricity was supplied by five turbogenerators (four of 460 kWt and one with a capacity of 230 kWt) and four reserve generators (one of 350 kWt and three of 150 kWt each). The total output of the ship's power plant was 2,870 kWt.

In the meantime, the Germans obtained information about the cruisers 26 and 26bis built in the USSR, with a main battery of 180 mm guns. Therefore, the expected "special circumstances" arose. On 14 November 1936, the decision was made to complete both cruisers as heavy, with 203 mm model C/34 guns[2]. This was a significant change, because the 203 mm guns fired 122 kg rounds with a range of up to 33,500 m, while the 150 mm guns fired only 45.5 kg rounds and had a range of 25,700 m. This was reflected in their armour piercing ability. The number of guns changed, instead of four three-barrel turrets, four twin-barrelled ones were installed. The redesign was not a major problem, because it concerned a small number of elements. The "Seydlitz" received an additional three rangefinders with a base of seven metres. One of them was replaced by a 6-metre rangefinder, and two additional ones were located in the two upper turrets of the main battery. Aviation equipment also changed. Only one catapult located behind the funnel and three seaplanes were planned for the "Seydlitz". The problem was to fit this into the permissible displacement of 10,000 tons. It turned out to be impossible, but the Kriegsmarine supreme command was not bothered. Ultimately, this parameter reached 14,000 tons. However, false information about the displacement of new ships within the limits of 10,000-10,600 tons had been made public.

On 18 July 1936, the Kriegsmarine placed the order for the construction of the cruiser at the Deschimag shipyard in Bremen. The construction cost was 84,090,000 RM.

Construction of the "Seydlitz"

The keel under the K cruiser was laid on 29 December 1936 (construction No. 940) at the Aktien-Gesellschaft "Weser" shipyard (Deschimag A.G.) in Bremen. At the end of 1938, shortly before launching the hull, the Germans decided to officially inform His Majesty's government about the construction of the K cruiser and its sister ship named with the letter L. The launch took place on 19 January 1939 and was combined with the naming ceremony. The ship was named "Seydlitz" in memory of the great Prussian General Friedrich Wilhelm Seydlitz (1721-1773), a cavalryman and hero of the Seven Years' War, serving under the orders of Frederic the Great. The cruiser was the second ship thus named. Her predecessor - the battlecruiser "Seydlitz" - took part in the most important naval engagement of the First World War - the Jutland Battle, and ended her career in Scapa Flow, where she was scuttled on 21 June 1919. Adm. Richard Foerster, a gunnery officer on her predecessor, became the master at the launching ceremony, and the godmother of the vessel was the widow of Commander von Egida, the skipper of the cruiser in 1913.

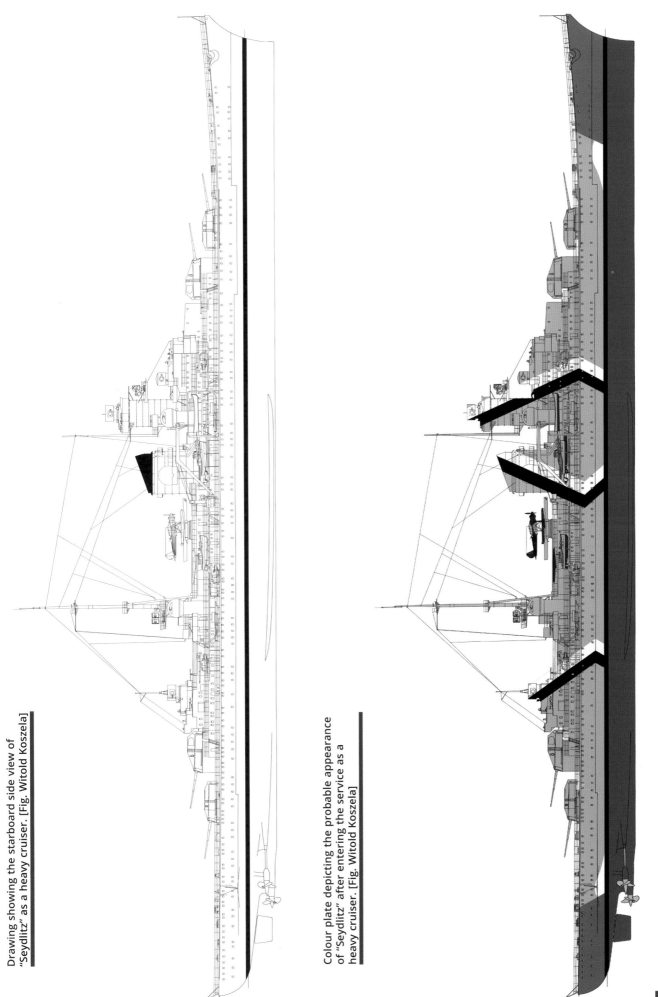

Drawing showing the starboard side view of "Seydlitz" as a heavy cruiser. [Fig. Witold Koszela]

Colour plate depicting the probable appearance of "Seydlitz" after entering the service as a heavy cruiser. [Fig. Witold Koszela]

The "K" type cruiser on the slipway of the Deschimag shipyard in Bremen before the launching ceremony - at the beginning of 1939.

The "Seydlitz" slides off the slipway of the Dechimag shipyard in Bremen, next to a cheering crowd.

The outbreak of the Second World War found the "Seydlitz" in the process of fitting out, the technical readiness of the cruiser was then estimated at 66.5%, and the completion of work was planned for early 1941. As already mentioned, both the "Seydlitz" and the next cruiser "Lützow" were built like "Prinz Eugen", initially assuming that they would be armed with 150 mm guns.

Allied paperchase

The signing of the Ribbentrop-Molotov Pact on 23 August 1939 opened a new chapter in the cooperation of both regimes[3]. Mutual relations strengthened even more after the attack of the two powers on Poland and, in fact, the fourth partition of Poland. The war unleashed by Hitler accompanied by Stalin gave an additional impulse to mutual relations. The Soviet Union provided the Germans with strategic raw materials (including oil, nonferrous metals and cereals) needed for the war, in exchange Germany offered their ally access to the latest military technologies. The authorities in the Soviet Union, as suggested by the naval specialists, expressed interest in the purchase of large surface ships, including heavy cruisers. The Soviet Economic Commission residing in Germany in October 1939 talked to their hosts about the sale of both cruisers and the help of German specialists in their completion. On 4 November 1939, an official offer was made for the purchase of two Blucher class vessels being built: the "Seydlitz" and "Lützow". On 7 December the Soviets expressed their desire to purchase the third cruiser of this series - "Prinz Eugen". The Soviet Union was hoping for a successful finalization of the negotiations, which was supported by circumstances, even the perceived lack of manpower for the completion of these ships.

On 22 November 1939, a joint committee meeting of representatives of the Naval ministries, shipbuilding and weapons industries of the USSR took place, during which the intention of purchasing military technology and weapons in Germany was considered. Among others, on the advisability of buying the heavy cruisers "Seydlitz" and "Lützow". Naval experts drew attention to the advantages of these ships: powerful guns exceed-

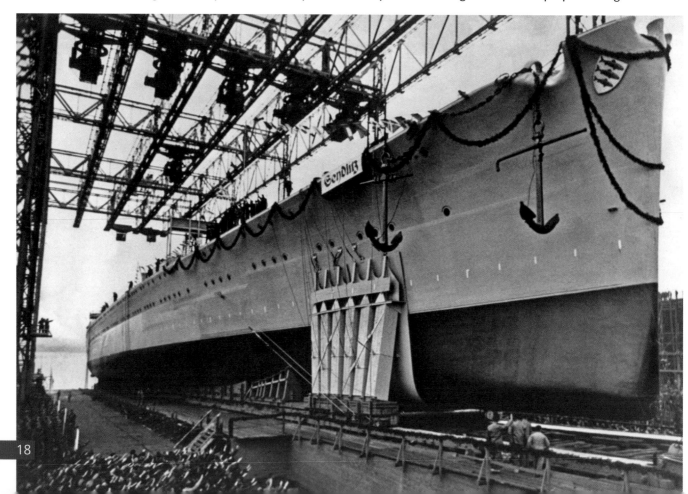

ing the armament of the Soviet Project 68 cruisers, stabilized secondary guns, inclined 80 mm broadside armour, the equivalent of a hundred-millimetre armour and longitudinal anti-torpedo bulkhead. Also mentioned were the cons: weak armour of the decks, the linear design of the engine arrangement and high parameters of steam, raising doubts as to the reliability of the engine[4]. After a long hesitation, Hitler finally refused to allow the sale of the three cruisers. In January 1940 he accepted the withdrawal of only one of the last of the cruiser series - "Lützow". After the refusal of the sale in November 1939, work on the "Seydlitz" resumed. As military operations at sea developed, the pace of work on the ship was falling as the expansion of the U-boot fleet became a priority. The originally planned deadline for commissioning the ship was not kept. By May 1942, the main armament was installed on the cruiser and all superstructures were assembled. There was still the installation of anti-aircraft weapons left, aircraft equipment (catapult, hangar and cranes), as well as masts and fire control devices. The ship's technical readiness at this point reached 90%, and according to some publications (Gröner) even 95%. Nevertheless, in July this year, the fitting out works were interrupted. Hitler's growing frustration over the losses suffered by the heavy Kriegsmarine ships made him less and less enthusiastic about the surface vessels.

The "Weser-1" project

The results of the German raids by heavy warships failed Hitler's expectations. After the loss of "Bismarck" in May 1941, he issued a clear order that the major ships would not enter combat until the enemy aircraft carriers were eliminated. The raids of ships from bases in Norway against British convoys going to Russia gave a bitter spell. Hitler went berserk and demanded the immediate withdrawal of all the major surface ships from service. During a discussion with Admiral E. Raeder, he stated that the large ships no longer had any operational value and that they should be removed from service, and that their guns would be used on land[5].

The Kriegsmarine supreme command had been convinced for some time about the necessity of having air cover while operating ships away from their home bases. The first aircraft carrier (the "Graf Zeppelin") began to be built in 1936. The situation in 1942 prompted a search for other concepts of using heavy ships. One of the first decisions taken was the resumption of work on the aircraft carrier "Graf Zeppelin" discontinued in 1940. Design work was carried out on new types of aircraft carriers, and existing vessels were sought for conversion into ships of this class. The choice fell, strangely, on the cruiser "Seydlitz", which in only a few months should have joined the

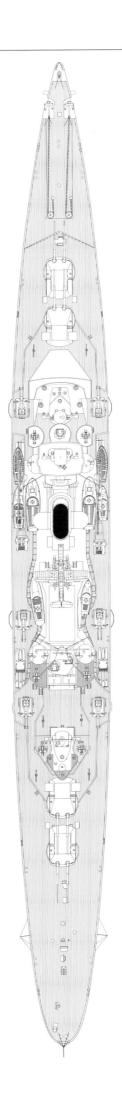
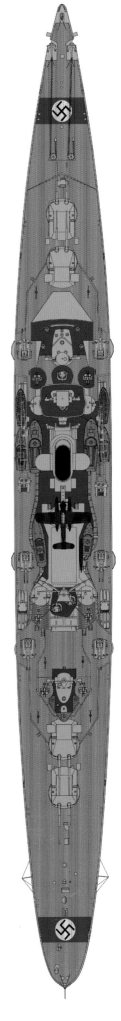

Top view of the "Seydlitz" as a heavy cruiser with four 2-gun 203 mm main battery turrets. [Fig. Witold Koszela]

Baptism ceremony of the "Seydlitz". From the right: Admiral Foerster, Admiral E. Roeder, Admiral K. Dönitz (?) and godmother of the ship, Mrs. von Egida.

Takeoffs, as in the case of the aircraft carrier "Graf Zeppelin", were to take place only with the help of two catapults placed in the fore section of the flight deck with a 22 m track. The landing planes had four braking lines at their disposal, the first at a distance of about 39.0 m from the edge of the aircraft deck, the last - 82.50 m.

The gun armament was to consist of five twin-barrel dual-purpose 105 mm L/65 C/31 guns on five C/33 mounts with an ammunition supply of 4,000 rounds; five twin-barrel 37 mm L/83 C/30 cannons on five C/30 mounts with a total stock of 16,000 rounds and six quadruple 20 mm L/65 C/38 cannons on C/38 mounts with a supply of 40,000 rounds. The main weapon of the aircraft carrier was supposed to be the on-board planes. The aviation group for the "Seydlitz" was to be made up of aircraft of the same type as those prepared for the aircraft carrier "Graf Zeppelin". These were the naval versions of two well-known Luftwaffe aircraft: Messerschmitt Bf 109 fighter planes and Junkers Ju 87 dive bombers. In connection with the decision to build aircraft carriers for the Kriegsmarine, Messerschmitt was given the task of constructing a special version of the Bf 109 fighter, which was developed in 1938 on the basis of Bf 109B. In the winter of 1939/1940, two prototypes (V.17 and V.17A) passed tests on an improvised artificial deck. These were Bf 109B, temporarily adapted for this purpose, but they showed a number of drawbacks. On 26 March 1940, a new prototype was tested, this time based on the Bf 109E. In 1942, it was used for tests with a catapult. It received the designation Bf 109T-1. In comparison with the Bf 109E it had an increased wing area as well as wing span. The aircraft did not have a wing folding mechanism, but it was possible to remove the wings from the fuselage manually, as in any version of Bf 109. The landing gear was also strengthened. Between the fifth and

fleet. But it happened differently. Initially, which is not surprising, it caused violent opposition from the command of the Kriegsmarine. In the end, the conviction won that an aircraft carrier was more needed than one more heavy ship. On 26 August 1942, the final decision was made.

Initial design work under the codename "Weser-1" was carried out from May 1942. On 18 August 1942, the design for the conversion into an aircraft carrier was presented. Hitler approved it on 26 August that year. The project envisaged a continuous aircraft deck with a length of 197 metres and a width of 30 metres (of which 22 metres could be used for air operations). Below the deck there was a hangar able to accommodate 20 machines (according to other data 18) and two central elevators for lowering and raising aircraft measuring 12.5 by 12.5 m. The aircraft carrier's air group consisted of 10 Messerschmitt Bf 109G fighter planes (according to other data Bf 109T) and the same number of Junkers Ju 87D dive bombers (according to other data Ju 87C).

The "Seydlitz" at the dockside of the Deschimag shipyard in 1941.

Tab. 3. The Messerschmitt Bf 109T specification.	
Parameter	
Dimensions, m	
length, wing span, height	8.8/11.10/ 2.60
Wing surface, m2	17.50
Weight, kg	
empty	2,000
normal	2,800
max.	3,080
Engine, number × output, HP	1 × 1,200
Max. speed, km/h	
at an altitude	572
at the ground	487
economical	440–450
Raising speed, m/s	17
Range, km	910
Crew	1
Armament	
guns × calibre mm, type	2 × 20 MG FF, 2 × 7.92 MG 17
bombs	4 × SC 50 or 1 × SC 250*

* Applies to the T2 variant.

sixth frames of the fuselage, a catapult clamping attachment was installed. There was a landing hook in the tail section of the fuselage. The T-2 subvariant had racks fitted under fuselage for installation of 300-litre fuel tanks, four SC 50 bombs or one SC 250 bomb (see Table No. 3).

The design of the on-board bomber was developed on the basis of a standard Ju 87B and in March-April 1939 two Ju 87B-1 planes were converted. This is how the Ju 87C ("Cäsar") was created, differing in that it had catapult and landing hook fittings and manually-folded wings. Their wing span was increased to 13.19 m. The width of the machine with folded wings was 5 m (the same as the span of the horizontal fin). In order to increase the flight range, a 300-litre fuel tank and an additional 48-litre oil tank were provided. In the wing panels there are inflatable bladders increasing buoyancy in the event of an emergency landing on water. An inflatable boat and rescue equipment were placed in the tail part. The main innovation was to blow off the landing gear, so that the aircraft would not capsize when trying to land on the water. A pre-series of ten Ju 87C-0s was produced in the summer of 1939. The Ju 87C-I was planned to be equipped with a hydraulic wing folding system, torpedo racks or under-fuselage bombs and under-wing tanks. Since the construction of the aircraft carrier "Graf Zeppelin" was discontinued, the production of the Ju 87C-1 was also suspended, and the aircraft produced were transformed into regular Ju 87B-Is. In 1942, work on a dive bomber version of the Ju 87E ("Emil") was resumed briefly. (see Table No. 4).

The initial calculation indicated large costs of conversion of the cruiser into an aircraft carrier. It was to last two years and absorb about 3,000 tons of materials, mainly high-grade steel and, what is equally important, it required the involvement of as many as 1,400 employees. However, before the reconstruction began, it was necessary to dis-

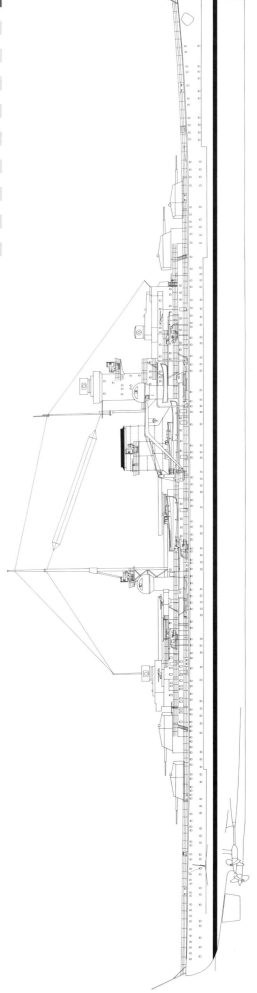

A drawing showing the starboard side view of the "Seydlitz" as a light cruiser with four three-barrelled 150 mm gun turrets. [Fig. Witold Koszela]

The aft part of the cruiser's hull with the barbette of the 203 mm turret visible - late 1939.

mantle the almost finished ship to the main deck level. The first thing was to disassemble the super-structure and remove the main gun turrets. At the beginning of December 1942, disassembly was virtually completed. In total, structures weighing 2,400 tons were removed. The largest object left on the upper deck of the cruiser was a massive funnel, which was to be moved to the starboard side of the ship. Now it was necessary to change the structure of the hull above the armoured belt. The remodelling project envisaged two additional levels of the hull (partly open from the broadsides) accommodating a narrow aircraft hangar. But at this point the career of "Seydlitz" as an aircraft carrier was discontinued. In January 1943 Hitler issued an order to stop the reconstruction of the cruiser into an aircraft carrier. During 1943, noth-

The "Seydlitz" in Königsberg in 1945.

ing happened on the ship, all the time she was moored to the quay of the Deschimag shipyard in Bremen. The turrets with 203 mm guns were transported and installed in the shore fortifica-tions near Lorient.

Operation "Ritter" ("Knight")

The ever-increasing threat of air raids by Allied planes forced the Kriegsmarine's command to make the decision to relocate the ship's hull to a safer place. The choice fell on Konigsberg, which was beyond the reach of bombers. Although the deci-sion was made at the end of 1943, the "Seydlitz" remained in Bremen for the following months. The reason was the lack of tugs. In addition, the winter of 1943/1944 was extremely cold, and the freez-ing of the southern part of the Baltic Sea continued until the end of the first quarter of 1944. It was not until 30 March of this year that the "Ritter" operation began. The tugs "Memmert", "Rixhöft" and "Movensteert" towed the unfinished hull of the would-be aircraft carrier to Kiel. From there the group, preceded by the icebreaker "Pollux", arrived in Königsberg on 2 April. At the new base, the fitting out work was practically not resumed. There was a shortage of engineers and technical staff, material difficulties were also great. In addi-tion, the Germans now had other worries than the construction of aircraft carriers. The ship's hull was a floating barracks until the end of the year. At the beginning of January 1945, a ring of encirclement by Soviet troops was tightened around Königsberg. All ships capable of putting to sea and of being used in the war were evacuated from the port of Königsberg. The "Seydlitz", however, remained in place, perhaps because of her size. On 29 January 1945, the ship was towed to the part of the port for handling timber, where a special team of engineers scuttled her to the bottom, detonating explosives and opening the kingstons. Konigsberg stood, however, and the counteroffensive of the German army forced back the Soviets for 20-30 km and restored the connection with Pilau. The sea passage was unblocked and evacuation continued. At the end of February, however, the Kriegsmarine headquarters decided to tow "Seydlitz" to Kiel to dismantle her to use as a source of spare parts. However, it was too late, a special team investigating the possibility of lifting the wreck showed it was hopeless. On 10 April 1945, Konigsberg surrendered, and the victorious Red Army occupied the port and captured the wrecks, including the "Seydlitz".

A fire to "honour" Stalin

The "Seydlitz" had settled on the bottom at a depth of 7.7 m at the bow and 10 m at the stern. Because the ship's height was from 10.15 to 12.45 m, most areas were flooded. Two weeks after the occupation of Konigsberg (24 April 1945), work was undertaken to lift the wreck from the bottom. A team of divers from the 75th Detachment of the South Baltic Fleet (EPRON) - an organization specialized in underwater work which had previously raised the sister cruiser "Petropavlovsk" - began with sealing the hull. On 25 May 1945, the ship was raised. She had spent almost four months on the bottom[6].

Although the ship was not officially mentioned in a fleet listing, a full-time crew of 366 men was set up and an improvised ship's company was formed. There was a chronic shortage of personnel, so there were also men from other branches of the armed forces among the crew members. As of 4 December 1945, there were actually only 230 of them. The duty of commander of the ship was at that time handed over to the commander of the Fifth Department, Eng. Captain of the 3rd Rank Artyom Fedorovich Sviridov. Later, he was replaced by Captain of the 2nd Rank, Alexandr Konstantinovich Pavlovsky[7]. Immediately after lifting the ship, the hastily assembled crew began cleaning the ship's quarters and simple maintenance of the mechanisms. The work went slowly, and in addition on the 20th (according to other data the 30th) December 1945, a fire broke out in the fore part of "Seydlitz". For the first time this event was described as late as in 2003 in the "Baltiyskaya Gazeta" published in Kaliningrad. An article by V. Pitchugin describing the post-war fate of the "Seydlitz" appeared in it.

Aerial view of "Seydlitz" at the fitting out quay of the Deschimag shipyard in Bremen - May 1942.

The author relied on the account of an eyewitness - a resident of the village of Novaya Kacheyevka (Mordovia) Semen Tereshkin, who just after the war served on the captured cruiser. Tereshkin was mobilized at the end of the war. He served with the Special Branch of the Baltic Fleet[8]. According to his account, the fire occurred on 20 December 1945. In connection with the approaching anniversary of Stalin's birth, a meeting was organised on the ship[9]. There was also an orchestra taken from a nearby POW camp (!?). Here is Tereshkin's account: *I had just washed and gone to bed. Suddenly, around midnight, there was an action stations signal. I jumped from the third level to the berth. I jumped onto the deck. Here the first explosion was heard. Flames everywhere. We had to tow the ship away from the pier, but how? The mechanisms had already been preserved. The junior technician, Lieutenant Semen Roshal, shouts: what are we going to do now? I tell him - there is a huge tree on the shore. We will hook on the rope and pull the anchor lift. Will the tree stand it? I answer that it should.* Meanwhile, the fire grew stronger. In order not to let it spread, things were being thrown out of the cabins. Expensive German furniture and a piano were thrown into the sea. Then came the second, most deafening explosion. Tereshkin lost consciousness. He woke up after 17 hours. The fire has already been extinguished. And the ship's doctor Shokhman was leaning over Semyon: *Well, lad, you're not supposed to die yet. You will live!*

Tereshkin's account raises some doubts (the fragment with a rope and a tree) and surprise (a German orchestra aboard the cruiser), But it is

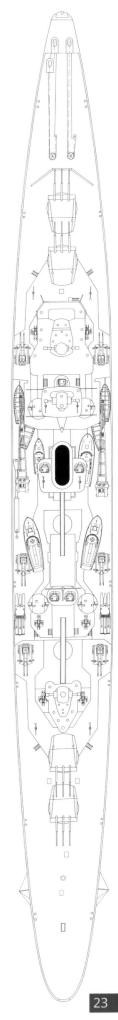

Top view of the "Seydlitz" as a light cruiser with four three-barrelled 150 mm turrets. [Fig. Witold Koszela]

Tab. 4. The Ju 87C-1 dive bomber specification	
Parameter	
Dimensions, m	
length, wing span, height	11.00/13.20/3.77
Wing surface, m²	31.30
Weight, kg	
empty	2,900 (3,655)
normal	4,510 (4,800)
max.	– (5,350)
Engine, number × output, HP	1 × 1,200
Max. speed, km/h	
at an altitude	380 (344)
at the ground	650
economical	306 (296)
Climbing speed, m/min	226 (3.7 m/s)
Range, km	1,160 (800)
Practical altitude, m	8000
Crew	2
Armament	
guns, × number, calibre, mm, type	2 × 7.92 MG 17, 1 × 7.92 M 15
bombs	1× 500 kg or 1 × 250 + 4 × 50

The "Seydlitz's" hull after launching, port side anti-torpedo bulges are clearly visible.

difficult to question the very fact of a fire. It was so strong that there was the threat of explosion of the cruiser's "oil tanks". The plating of the port side in the surface from the bow stem on the length of 80 frames was bulged and had breaches. An analogous phenomenon occurred with the top, middle and bottom deck plating at a distance of five metres from the ship's broadside. In the area of the second main battery turret, bulges were created over the entire width of the hull. The broadside armour plates from the fore traverse towards the bow were deformed and apparently lost their mechanical properties. A barge (a tugboat?) which supplied heat to the cruiser also sank. The reason was the explosion of the boiler, which was flooded with cold water? Something (or someone) must have knocked out a hole in the hull of the barge? According to Semnen Tereshkin, 78 men were killed, and buried in a big trench excavated by a bulldozer. Three victims are officially talked about: Sgt. 1ˢᵗ Rank N. F. Vyerin, ratings E. P. Ivanov and V. S. Romanov. They are currently buried in a common grave at the intersection of the Mir and Engels Streets in Kaliningrad. In some reports, a fourth fire victim appears - rating E. K. Vereshchinskyi, whose name is not mentioned on the memorial plaque of the monument. There were no boiler room staff among the victims. Three of the fallen were in the engine

room at the position of a diesel generator. Perhaps the fire broke out in the engine room. From the accounts of those who survived, Teereshkin learned about the verdict of the military tribunal and the execution of the skipper of "Seydlitz" Pavlovskyi and the head of the electromechanical section of the cruiser. They were accused of cooperation with the Germans. Tereshkin describes the commander as a calm officer, who read much and who did not establish close relations with the crew, but he had a sentiment towards the Germans. Official sources do not confirm the fact of the officers being shot. At least until 20 February 1946, they were still officially in their positions, and they were also awarded the medals "For victory over Germany in the Great Patriotic War"[10].

A troublesome war booty

Despite the damage caused by the fire, a special commission appointed by the naval commander Admiral N. G. Kuznetsov, assessed the technical condition (combat readiness) of the ship in the area of the electromechanical section at 85%, and generally at 60-65%. At the same time, specialists noted that the general state of "Seydlitz" was better than the state of the "Tallin" (ex "Petropavlovsk", ex "Lützow"). There was a proposal to introduce "Seydlitz" into the service before "Tallin", even without regard to the fact that the ship was deprived of almost all its superstructures. A large amount of furniture and other equipment were found in the ship's stores. The forecastles and cabins were fully furnished. Likewise, there were toilets and washrooms, laundries and bathrooms. There were boilers and cold stores in the messes and the caboose. The ship's storerooms were fully equipped. The officer's cabins above the water level were in perfect condition. The ammunition magazines were also fully equipped with all safety systems, only the racks were missing. The most important thing, however, was that the engine was almost completely assembled, only some auxiliary mechanisms in the boiler rooms were missing. In the engine compartment, a set of diesel motors and turbogenerators was found. Most importantly, the power unit, despite flooding, was in very good condition, even the boilers (preserved by the Germans) did not suffer much. In a top-secret report it was said that of the equipment which was installed on the aircraft carrier, the Soviet engineers had been working for many years. There were six giant bronze propellers on the upper deck, covered with wood. There were bundles of cable lines there in the armoured pipes from the dismantled superstructures, arranged and described in a specific order. On the deck was also the barbette of the second main battery turret removed from the hull. The worst problem was with electric motors and their equipment. After a four-month stay under water, the ship's power unit required a complete refurbishment. Similarly the

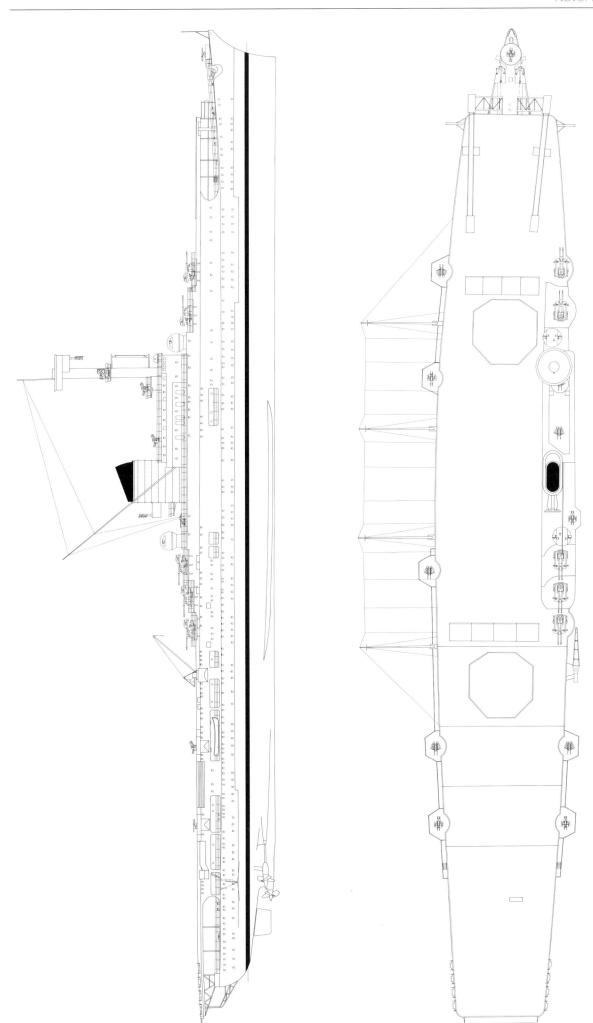

Drawings depicting the profile and top view of the "Seydlitz" as an aircraft carrier (Project "Weser-1"). [Fig. Witold Koszela]

ship. In the prisoner-of-war camps, about 1,000 German ship engineers and specialist technicians were found. Plans to complete the cruiser received a "blessing" even from the deputy defence minister General of the Army N. A. Bulganin. However, the euphoria associated with the project of reconstruction of the cruiser slowly decreased, and the army of opponents of this idea grew rapidly. The first protested to the head of the Central Scientific and Research Institute of Shipbuilding (CNII) of the fleet Eng. Rear-Adm. N. V. Alexeyev. He pointed out that after completing the "Seydlitz" the fleet would receive a unique ship, the only one with such a power unit and atypical weaponry, without the necessary spare parts. Installation of domestic anti-aircraft weapons and fire control devices (of large dimensions and weight) would cause problems with the stability of the ship. The Admiral suggested that efforts should focus on completing the aircraft carrier "Graf Zeppelin". The idea of completing the German cruiser also did not appeal to the representatives of the shipbuilding industry. The construction office of the Baltic Shipyard was overwhelmed with work on the projects for the local cruisers Project 68K and 68bis. If the shipyard were to deal with "Seydlitz", there would be serious delays in the design and construction of these cruisers. All these problems, however, were nothing when compared to the most important issue: no main guns were available. By the order of Admiral N. G. Kuznetsov, all German naval bases seized by Soviet troops were searched. Equipment, material, spare parts and documents necessary to complete the ship were sought. In spite of all these efforts, no new 203 mm guns were found in Germany, nor the turrets for them, which was very important. In this situation, there could be no question of the completion of both ships. Therefore, in September 1946, a new idea appeared to complete the cruiser with Soviet 180 mm guns in three-barrelled turrets. The idea turned out to be a failure, because the MK-3-180 turrets were no longer produced, and the resumption of their production required two to two and a half years. Meanwhile, the "Seydlitz" since 30 October remained at Shipyard No. 189 and waited for the green light to commence completion. It was not until February 1947 that the General Staff of the Soviet Navy decided to equip the cruiser with 152 mm guns in MK-5 turrets and 100 mm general-purpose guns in SM-5 turrets. The ship's completion schedule was also established: engine trials - third quarter of 1948, completion of the ship - fourth quarter of 1949. The plan was dropped in a month. In addition to the aforementioned difficulties, the allies pressed the Russians to scuttle both "Seydlitz" and "Graf Zeppelin" or dismantle them for scrapping in accordance with the agreement

The "Seydlitz" - January 1940, assembly of the funnel (still without the cover) and a mast.

hull. In addition to the consequences of the fire, it was necessary to repair a few large holes in the anti-torpedo bulges. All transverse bulkheads did not show signs of damage and were in good condition. In this situation, the committee's proposal could only be one: the "Seydlitz" was to be completed, but as a heavy cruiser, because the Soviet leadership had a special aversion to aircraft carriers. The ship was decided to be towed to Leningrad and converted again at the Shipyard No. 189. Then she was to be completed together with her sister

The "Seydlitz" during fitting out works - January 1940.

of the tripartite commission for the division of the German fleet.

Yet another sinking

On 19 March 1947, the Council of Ministers of the USSR, in connection with the commitments accepted at the Potsdam Conference, decided to scuttle the German ships of the so-called group "C". The surface ships included the cruiser "Seydlitz" and the aircraft carrier "Graf Zeppelin". Urgent disassembly of devices and mechanisms, as well as other elements that could be removed, was initiated. On 20 August, the disassembly was completed, after three days the ship was handed over to the scuttling unit. After this operation, the displacement of "Seydlitz" decreased to 7,100 t, and the average draft to 3.5 m. On 24 August 1947, the ship was towed to the designated area and sunk in the waters of the Gulf of Finland after detonating explosive charges.

The last commander of the ship was the Captain of the 1st Rank Vasily Dmitrievich Vinogradov. Many Western publications, as well as modern Russian ones, give incorrect information about scrapping the ship in 1947 (according to others it was to remain even until 1958). One of the more well-known authors, A. B. Shirokorad, mentions the projects of 1951 to create from two ships ("Tallin" and "Seydlitz") one school ship with the following weapons: 12 × 152 mm, 8 × 130 mm and a smaller calibre guns. If such a project was created, it had to affect only one ship - "Tallin", because the second one had for four years rested on the bottom of the Baltic Sea.

SOURCE OF PHOTOS: S. BREYER, DIE SCHWEREN KREUZER DER SEYDLITZ – KLASSE. „MARINE ARSENAL" BAND 22. 1993; WUERTTEMBERGISCHEN LANDESBIBLIOTHEK, STUTTGART

Bibliography

Berezhnoy S. S., *Trofei i reparatsii VMF SSSR*, Yakutsk 1994.

Breyer S., *Die schweren kreuzer der Seydlitz – klasse* [In:] "Marine Arsenal" 1993, Band 22.

Gröner E., *Die deutschen kriegsschiffe 1815–1945*, Band 1. Bonn 1998.

Yakimov S. A., *Khronika shturma Pillau*, Kaliningrad 2007.

Kofman W., *Tiazhelye kreysera tipa Admiral Hipper*, Moscow 1996.

Koop G., Schmolke K-P., *Die schweren kreuzer der Admiral Hipper – klasse*, Bonn 1992.

Nowarra Heinz J., *Die Deutsche Luftrüstung 1933–1945*, Bernard & Graefe Verlag, Koblenz 1993.

Pacholski Ł., *Krążowniki ciężkie typu Admiral Hipper* [In:] "Morze Statki i Okręty" 2011, No. 12.

Perepeczko A., *Niemieckie krążowniki typu Admiral Hipper, cz. 1*, "Encyklopedia okrętów wojennych", No. 33, Gdańsk 2004.

Platonov A. V., *Germanskey tyazhelye kreysery pod sowietskim flagom* [In:] "Gangut" 2006, No. 37.

Szirokorad A. B., *Wielikaja Kontribucjia. Czto SSSR połuczył poslie wojny*, Moskwa 2013.

Trojca H. i W., *Krążowniki ciężkie klasy Admiral Hipper*, Warsaw 1993.

"Baltiyskaya Gazeta", Vol. 2003.

Website: http://forum-kenig.ru (access: 10.11. 2017).

Endnotes

1. On 9 July 1935, Germany issued a declaration on the construction of two heavy cruisers (the construction of one of them began already on 6 July).

2. Because eight three-barrelled turrets with 150mm calibre guns and two sets of fire control devices intended for these ships were already in production, they were intended to be sold to the USSR to arm two of the Project 68 cruisers in construction since 1939. According to other data, it was only four turrets (work on them was carried out until the end of 1941).

3. Military cooperation of both countries had been developing since the USSR was established in 1922, and its early beginnings date back to 1917.

4. S. I. Titushkin, Tyazhelyi kreiser "Petropavlossk" [in:] "Sudostroyenye" 1996, Issue No. 5–6, p. 66.

5. E. M. Raeder, *Moje życie*, Gdańsk 2001, p. 478.

6. This is contradictory to the content of Order No. 178 of the Commander of the Baltic Fleet of 22 December 1945: "[...] C. (comrade) Popov, being the commander of the diving group [...], in the period from 24 April to June 1945, participated in lifting the cruiser "Seydlitz". Many publications give the date of lifting the wreck in 1946.

7. Capt. of the 2nd Rank, A. K. Pavlowskyi commanded the cruiser "Petropavlovsk" (ex "Lützow") in 1941-1943.

8. The Special Branch of the Baltic Fleet numbered 60 people, divided into 10-person sub-units. Each of them had a military investigator. Tereshkin initially operated in Poland and probably dealt with the Polish resistance.

9. Stalin was born on 6 December 1878. There is much controversy around this date, also 9 December 1879 is given. To top it off, in 1929, a great celebration of his 50th birthday was held, which took place on December 21!

10. On some Internet forums you can find one more report from the fire on the "Seydlitz". A certain man named Rubtsov, who served on this ship, describes a fire that took place in the summer and was started while loading barrels of fuel onto the ship. The fire described in the text is contradictory to the season of the year and circumstances. Either another fire actually occurred, or Rubtsov confabulates.

"Seydlitz" - assembly of superstructures with help of a floating crane.

Casablanca type

The CVE-61 during the Battle of Leyte Gulf.

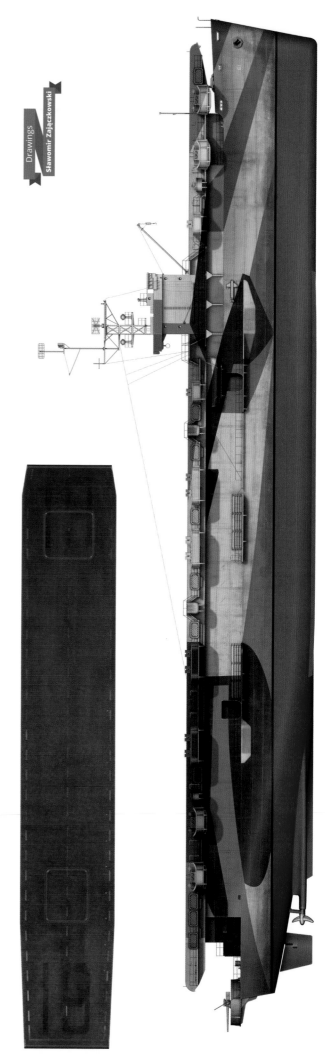

Drawings

Sławomir Zajączkowski

The CVE-64 sporting the Atlantic camouflage pattern of 1944.

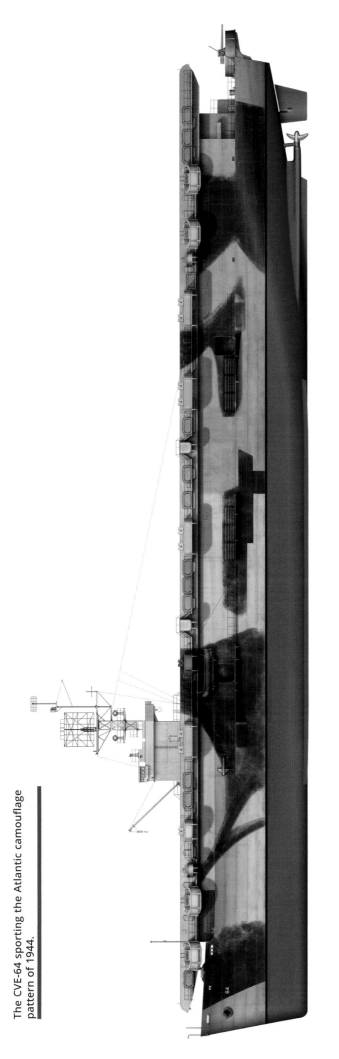

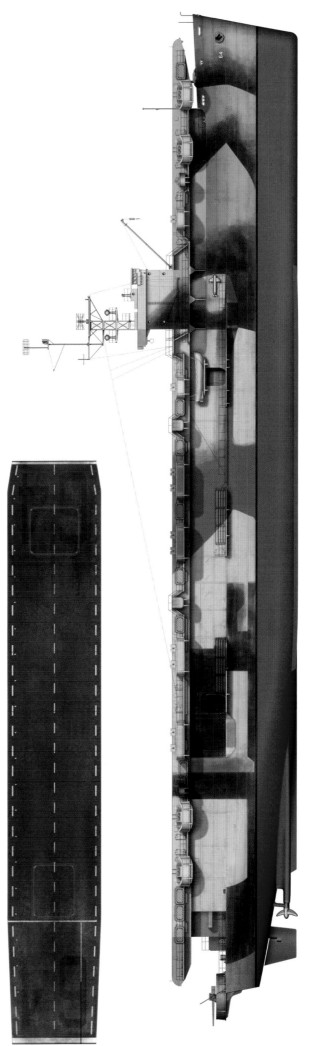

U-481 In The Gulf Of Finland

Mirosław Jastrzębski

The emblem of the U-481's conning tower. July 1944.

U-boats are usually associated with wolf packs and large convoy battles, or hunting alone for Allied shipping, torpedoing large ships in the endless waters of the Atlantic and their commanders awarded for such achievements with high decorations. The U-boat war was very different in the shallow, coastal waters of the small basin of the Gulf of Finland. Here, the U-boats, performing atypical tasks of mine lying and guarding vast minefields against hostile minesweepers, closely cooperated with land forces - with the naked eye watching the course of battles fought on land. During the last months of the war, the German Navy, including the U-Bootwaffe, played a special role in supplying and evacuating troops and civilians by sea, when it was no longer possible to be carried out by land.

Toward the Gulf of Finland

On 10 November 1943, the ceremony of commissioning of the next Type VIIC U-Boot U-481 took place in Kiel. Her skipper became an officer with no experience in independent command of a ship,

Oblt. z. S. d. R. (reserve officer) Ewald Pick, LI (the chief mechanic) became Lt. Ing. Küsgen, I W.O. (watch officer) was Lt. Z.S. Bischoff and II WO became Obstrm. (senior helmsman) Sobing. During the following days in the Bay of Kiel, the first sea trials and submersion exercises were carried out, which was standard practice for ships that had just entered service. On 26 November, when the submarine was returning to Kiel from the next exercise (in the company of the escort "Bergen"), U-481 collided with the Swedish steamer „Korsö" sailing from Stockholm. The U-481 floated on the surface, „slow ahead" behind the escort, heading 230°. At one moment Oblt. Pick ordered to the rudder set 10° to the port side and make the 208° bearing to follow the course of the escort changing it. The „Korsö" steamer was approaching from the bow starboard side. The escort turned even further to the port side, onto a course of 188°. The U-Boot rudder was still at the 10° position (U-Boot had not yet entered the 208° course) when Pick ordered a sharp turn to the left, but the U-Boot turned right! The rudder position indicator showed „to starboard", the machine telegraph was at „2 × half back"! When the approaching steamer was only 80 m from the U-boat, Pick gave the order: *Everyone abandon ship!* When the first sailors jumped into the water, the ship was jerked by the machine moving into reverse. At that moment, the U-boat's bow hit the steamer's starboard side, and bent heavily. However, the rigid inner hull did not suffer any damage. The steamer stopped nearby with a large leak, near the Holtenau Lock (eastern sluice of the Kiel Canal). The U-481 after a week went east - to Danzig (Pol. - Gdańsk), where the damage was dealt with and further training of the crew near Pilau (Rus. - Baltiysk) and Hela (Pol. - Hel) began. Over the next few weeks, Pick made further mistakes, and as a result, he was transferred to the training ship U-708, while Oblt.z.S. Klaus Andersen, commanding U-708, took over the U-481. The crew accepted the change with relief. In this situation, the training commenced again, because it was necessary to acquaint the whole crew with the new skipper. In mid-April, after completing all the training stages, the U-Boot returned to Kiel. Here, important changes were made within a few days to the ship's company, the chief mechanic and senior helmsman were replaced, as well as new seamen trained in operating modern anti-aircraft weapons were assigned. As a result of these changes, the U-Boot had to be again directed to perform more exercises in the Gulf of Gdańsk. They were very intensive and were completed in record time - already at the end of May 1944, the U-481 returned to the shipyard in Kiel, joining a large group of U-boats waiting to be fitted with snorkel devices.

At the time when the Allied troops in the west began landing operation in Normandy, opening the so-called second front, and in the south they reached Rome, in the east the Red Army launched a successful offensive in Karelia (located between the Baltic Sea and White Sea - between Leningrad and Murmansk) against the Finnish troops allied with Germany. The loss of control over Finland by the Germans would lead to the loss of domination in the Baltic Sea and thus the deprivation of supply capabilities of the northern front, which in turn would quickly lead to the loss of Leningrad and the Narva regions and the entire Baltic Sea coastline which had been occupied so far. It would be impossible to maintain the supply of raw materials from Sweden and this would severely limit the possibilities to continue the tonnage warfare in the Atlantic. The Germans, fearing that the Finns would conclude a separate peace with the Soviets, decided to first demonstrate their support to the Finns by sending U-boats to the Gulf of Finland. In mid-June 1944, the F.d.U. Mitte based in the Polish port of Gdynia (its commanding officer at that time was a veteran of the Battle of the Atlantic, Captain Viktor Schütze, who had sunk 35 Allied

ships), decided to send U-481 and U-748 (Oblt. Roth) as well as U-1193 (Oblt. Guse) to the Tallinn area. In the Gulf of Finland, there were no such well-organized U-boat bases as in Germany, the commanders had to act more independently, so Oblt.z.S. Andersen was to be the head of the first three U-boats as "ä. K" (German: *ältester Kommandant* - the oldest commander). A little later, from 13 July, more U-boats were to arrive to the Bjoerkoe and Narva Bay areas: U-679, U-475, U-479, U-370, U-242, U-250 and U-348 and from August U-1001, U-745 and U-717.

At the entrance to the Gulf of Finland (in the Hanko area) and in its waters themselves from the summer of 1941, many mines had been laid on the approaches to the ports and islands - which caused huge losses among the Soviets retreating from the Baltic States. The Soviets, Germans and Finns had all been laying mines. In 1942, a number of mine barriers were laid between Tallinn and the Finnish Porkkala Perkala together with a system of underwater nets (against Soviet submarines), expanded in 1943 between the Estonian Naissaar Island (German name Nargen, used later in the text in accordance with German archives) and the Porkkala Peninsula. In addition, there were still also minefields in the Gulf of Finland from World War One. Therefore, navigation in the Gulf of Finland was very difficult and dangerous. Often, minefields were marked on the German maps only with approximate accuracy. The depth of water in the vicinity of the numerous islands and islets of the Finnish coast was not accurately determined either, so the German navigators used rather the Finnish maps instead of the German *Quadratkarte*.

Finally, on the night of 18/19 June 1944, Andersen received his first operational order: *on 19 June at 00.00 hrs set off at the highest speed to Reval* (Est. - Tallinn), *in the shallow waters, sail at limited speed. Report the passing of Libau* (Lat. - Liepaja) *and 22 degrees longitude east to the F.d.U. Mitte* [Viktor Schütze – author's note]. With a delay of one hour, interrupting the unfinished fitting out works, the U-481 put to sea from Kiel to the eastern Baltic, reaching Tallinn after a 27-hour journey. By radio, Andersen reported the arrival and readiness to take action. Four hours later, the other two U-boats arrived. On 22 June all of them were ordered to be ready to patrol - one by one, moving at low speed – a route to Helsinki and further east to Kotka: Andersen from 23 June, Guse and Roth from 26 June.

On 23 June at 08.00, the U-481 left Tallinn for Helsinki. In the morning of the following day, Andersen reported to the headquarters of the 9th Sicherungsdivision (rear security division, recently commanded by Rear-Admiral Böhmer), liaison officer of the navy and the captain of the port. He received detailed information about cleared routes, moorings, routes to patrol zones, as well as the general situation on the land front. He also received new orders: *One U-Boot goes to Narva Bay, the other two to the Gulf of Neva* [the Kronstadt area – author's note]. On 25 June at 03.00, the U-481 left Helsinki, to the east, to the Kotka area, with the task of reconnoitring the situation and reporting the results of the reconnaissance. The designated area was reached at 11.00. Andersen quickly noticed that only some selected routes were cleared (free of mines). In this operational region there were numerous shallows, and the bottom in many places was constituted by sharp rocks, so navigation had to be carried out very carefully, with continuous use of sonar. Radio transmissions were satisfactory down to a depth of 25 m. Only underwater operations were possible. At 19.00 the U-Boot was turning back wide, towards the Narva Bay and on 26 June, she moored in Tallinn. The commander passed all his comments to Viktor Schütze (the F.d.U. Mitte) by radio. He also proposed to operate together with Finnish submarines in the area to the east of the nets and mine barriers, as well as to assign the German speedboats for the action (Ger. - T-Boote) and destroyers. At the disposal of the 9th Sicherungsdivision were, among others, six modern T-Boots and six destroyers. He proposed that the next U-Boots going to the Gulf of Finland should arrive in Helsinki, because in Tallinn there was a major air threat at that time and a huge movement of German vessels supplying the ground forces. However, as a port of return, he proposed German harbours, much less endangered than Finnish ones.

The first patrol

In the morning of 5 July, the order came from Gdynia: *Transfer, Andersen to Kjevsalö* [small port about 50 nm east of Helsinki - author's note], *Guse* [U-1193 - author's note] *to Emsalö* [a small port also to the east, but the closer by half – author's note]. *Readiness to leave within six hours.* Both U-Boots loaded, among others, the camouflage nets necessary in order to hide during daylight among the numerous small islands over there. Departure from the port was agreed at 07.00 the next day. Three hours before putting to sea, another order arrived: *Andersen, Guse, both ships go to Kjevsalö, closer to the operational area. Patrol zones moved further east, with the task of probing underwater to the area between the Bjoerkoe Island and Lavansaari* [entrance to the Neva Bay - author's note]. According to the plan, at 07.00 both U-Boots left Tallinn. On the way, the radio operator received another message from Gdynia: *Andersen. The situation requires the U-Boats to operate east of the mine barriers as soon as possible.*

After a careful day-long journey, the small island of Nuokko was reached in the evening - a waiting area located on the Finnish coast, just east of Kotka. From this place, underwater probes were to be performed into the Neva Bay. In the morning, the ships were camouflaged and the day passed on. Shortly before midnight, the radio operator received an operational order (No. 1) from the 9th Sicherungsdivision HQ: *Convoy, area south of the island of Huovari. Attack in square 142C1 to 143C2, direction Kronstadt. Report the expected return time.* U-481 sailed on the surface at the fastest possible speed to a remote point of interception. After two and a half hours, at 01.50 on 9 July, she reached the destination, and continued further slowly on a southerly course. At 06.00, at a distance of 1 nm from the island of Narvi, Andersen dived the ship. At half-hourly intervals, a 10-minute observation through periscope was conducted. Patrol ships were observed many times. At 15.00 the U-Boot was located on the east side of the designated square. In the Neva Bay smoke was only occasionally seen. Listening was impeded, the speedboats' movement was heavy since dusk. Shortly after midnight, the U-481 was between two small forces of the surface ships shelling each other. At 04.20 she emerged onto the surface. Andersen watched the area for 1.5 hours, then dived his U-boat. He made notes in his log book (later radioed to Gdynia, to Viktor Schütze, then they were passed to all U-boat commanders operating in the Gulf of Finland):

U-Boat stayed for 26.5 hours under the water, travelling a distance of 51.3 nm with speeds: at 14.05 hours. KF (small ahead, speed approx. 6.1 knots), 12.13 hours. LF (slow ahead, approx. 9.6 knots), 00.11 hours HF (half-ahead, around 11 knots), 00.02 hours GF (large ahead, approx. 16.7 knots). The air composition was good up to 23 hours: carbon dioxide content between 1.8-2%. After the crew manned their action stations, the level increased to 2.5-2.8 percent, but the crew coped with it well. At the moment of surfacing, there were 3,800 Ah of electricity in the batteries. A ship in this area should not stay under water longer than 38-42 hours, for a distance of 35 Nm of underwater travel to the area. At noon you should start the return voyage to get there before the next night.

During the day, the movement of speedboats and motorboats only - I have not observed any targets and do not expect them in the future. Night underwater probes around Lavansaari Island and further to the Neva Bay towards Kronstadt give you the opportunity to encounter larger ships, but visibility through the periscope is bad, small speedboats and chasers are easy to go unnoticed.

On 11 July the U-481 stayed far away, near Kotka, preparing for the next mission - this time further, to the Bjoerkoe area. She set off in the evening at 20.00, travelling under the water. She hit the rocky bottom several times, crossing the designated area from the east and west. Andersen observed the movement of Soviet patrol boats and the work of minesweepers. He did not notice anything special and he turned back at midnight on 12/13 July. He travelled 32 nm under the water, the remaining distance on the surface. Just before entering the improvised base, with a marked depth of only 8.5 m on the map, at one point he did not stick to the precisely marked route and went aground. He did not manage to get out on his own and the U-1193 came to his aid. Fortunately, the U-Boot did not suffer any damage and in the afternoon she moored at the base. After a very short stop, in the evening at 20.15 she set off for another patrol, this time further south, near Narva. After three hours the U-481 dived, starting to operate in a dangerous area, with innumerable shallows, without sounding. The next day in the afternoon the submarine hit the bottom, as a result of which the conning tower emerged slightly above the water, but on the horizon there were no enemy ships at that time. Before midnight, the U-Boot surfaced and the return to base commenced. On 16 July, an air raid took place (estimated by Andersen as over 100 aircraft) on Kotka and Hamina. Three planes flew low over the island of Nuokko, near the moored, camouflaged U-Boots, not noticing them. Fire was not opened to avoid detection. In the evening, the U-481 set off for another underwater trip - again to the Bjoerkoe area - to the entrance to the Neva Bay. As before, again, there were a lot of patrol boats (also in close proximity). At one point, the U-Boot hooked an anti-submarine net. She dragged it behind her for a while, but finally, moving back, she managed to disentangle herself. On 17 July, before evening, Andersen began the return to base, from midnight going all the time on the surface.

On 18 July, another order was received from the HQ of the 9th Sicherungsdivision: *In the area of the Bay of Narva, all targets are to be attacked and sunk. In the Neva Bay perform observation primarily.*

On 19 July in the evening, the U-481 again set sail for a mission in the Bay of Narva. The next day at 19.00 she secretly approached two Soviet patrol boats, sailing very slowly near each other. Andersen fired a torpedo from the No. 3 tube from a distance of 500 m. The torpedo probably went too deep without hitting the target. After midnight, the U-Boot began returning to the island of Nuokko, going the first 39 nautical miles under water, continuing on the surface.

On the evening of 22 July, Andersen left towards Bjoerkoe, where, changing course continuously, he sighted only numerous patrol boats. The next day, on the way back, the 9th Sicherungsdivision HQ ordered Andersen to sail in Helsinki, where the mooring lines were thrown on 24 July at 10.00. There he received current instructions: *Strong enemy aviation forces us to secure the safety of shipping on the approach to Narva during the day. The U-Boots must be in surveillance positions during the day, giving way to minesweepers at night. Report any enemy force in the area and fight them; report the appearance of enemy landing force and fight it. Communications limited.* Four hours later, the

U-481 in Tallinn in the summer of 1944.

U-481 was returning to sea, to the area of Narva. At 02.00 she reached a position from where the battle raging on the land was visible to the naked eye. At 22.00 Andersen emerged and handed over the area to the commander of the 1st MS-Flottille (Mine-Sweeper Flotilla). At this time of year, the night in the Gulf of Finland lasts approx. 3.5 hours, so there was little time for U-Boats to charge batteries and ventilate the ship, as well as for the work of minesweepers. In this basin, the use of snorkels only solved to a limited extent the problem of recharging the energy in the batteries and ventilation of the interior due to the exhaust smoke visible from a distance, as well as the valve protruding above the water, easy to detect by planes. Andersen passed his comments to the headquarters in Gdynia on the first day of the operation: *Observation in the sector from 02.00. No special events. At noon, immersion for periscope observation and underwater listening. Visibility is good, dark lead-coloured clouds protect against detection from the air. Constant sounds of fighting. Square 94a. Andersen.* At the time, there were 12 U-boats in the Gulf of Finland.

In the afternoon of that day – 26 July – a drifting mine was sighted through the periscope of the U-481 submerged at a depth of 10 m. It was detonated by gunfire at the second attempt. After an hour another alarm - another mine, also detonated. At 22.00 the U-Boot withdrew 10 nm. Soon, a Soviet plane flying at 1,000 m was noticed. The engines were immediately stopped so that the wake would not reveal the presence of the submarine and the plane disappeared. The U-Boot remained in position. A few minutes before 02.00, already on 27 July, the plane appeared again - it was an Il-2 attack aircraft. It detected the U-boot and attacked at an altitude of 50 m from the starboard side, firing inaccurately too high. It turned around, circling, but was forced to stay on the edge of the fire range of the 2-centimetre anti-aircraft cannons. Ten minutes later, a second plane, already approaching, was noticed. U-481 performed an immediate, emergency dive. During the whole of the next day, nothing special happened. After 22.00 the ship surfaced. In front, to the background of artillery flashes from the coastline from the area of Narva, a group of minesweepers was sighted. Andersen made further comments for Viktor Schütze:

For the ship's safety, the following measures are necessary:

The ship should be stopped, keeping the bow in the direction of the best visibility.

Anti-aircraft weapons play a special role. They must be manned and ready to immediately open fire in every direction.

The normal battery charging time up to 1,400 Ah takes 3-4 hours.

The engine must be kept permanently ready for immediate movement.

This allows you to achieve: a) a stable weight due to low fuel consumption, b) there is no trace of the ship on the water. Today I detected from a distance of 6-7 m a force of minesweepers heading slowly 2 nm from the mainland.

The disadvantage of stopping the ship in the face of a sudden attack should be taken into account.

Successes of the first patrol

The U-481 retired from the position, giving way to minesweepers. At midnight U-481 was attacked by two fighter planes, but effective fire from the AA guns again prevented them approaching closer than 500 m. Planes tried again to get closer from the coast, using the flashes of artillery fire of ongoing fighting on land to blind the U-boot, but again, they were stopped by effective fire and finally withdrew to the east. The next hour was spent on alert, which delayed the two hours of battery charging, after which Andersen returned to position and submerged the ship to periscope depth (16 m) in order to spend on observation the entire day which was just beginning. As he noted - the ship was beautifully kept at this depth. The day passed without special events. At 23.00 the U-Boot surfaced and withdrew for three hours, giving way to the oncoming minesweepers. On 29 July in the evening, after surfacing, a drifting mine was detonated, while remaining in the sector. The shoreline was so smoky that for over a dozen hours it was impossible to check the position, the visibility was limited, so after charging the battery the U-Boot went under water. Immediately after she surfaced at 04.00, around 20-30 mines and two Soviet minesweepers at a distance of 1,200 m were sighted. Two hours later, at the bearing 80° increment, seven consecutive boats were approaching, heading west. After another 30 minutes, in the distance 20 more minesweepers appeared in the same sector. Suddenly there were three mine explosions between them. After a few minutes there were four fighter planes flying at 4,000 m. They circled and, diving, began their descent to attack. The crews of the U-boot's guns opened an effective fire, keeping the fighters away. After a dozen or so minutes of circling in the air, the fighters repeated their attempt to attack, again ineffectively, and then withdrew. Another 1.5 hours passed with the increased observation from the U-boot's bridge, all the time sharing the attention between the observation of the sky and remote enemy minesweepers, after which the U-boot dived. During the morning the minesweepers approached and moved away several times, soon they left.

Observing from periscope depth, at 15.30, a formation of about 20 boats at a bearing 30° was seen at a distance of 6,000 m, going west to the mine barrier hidden in the mist. Immediately, battle stations were ordered and the U-Boot moved at high speed to the north in order to reach a position favourable to the attack: between the barrier and the formation of ships. After an hour, fortunately for Andersen, the force changed course to the south (towards the coast) and after another 30 minutes it was at 190° and 7,000 m, approaching the U-Boot, leaving the foggy area. Andersen waited a few minutes and quickly fired a torpedo from a distance of 4,000 m from the bow tube at two overlapping targets, setting the depth of the torpedo track to 1 m. After 25 seconds there was an explosion. *An unknown type of vessel, with a narrow funnel, metal parts flew into the air in a cloud of black smoke* - as he noted in the log. The U-Boot quickly made a turn to fire the next torpedo from the stern tube, remaining at periscope depth, while the formation of ships began to scatter in panic. Five minutes after the first shot, Andersen suddenly saw two minesweepers heading towards the U-Boot. He quickly fired a torpedo from a distance of 4,000 m at three overlapping targets (at a large 104-degree angle) from the stern tube and descended to 18 m so that the trawl devices of the passing boats would not damage the U-Boot. After 1 min and 55 sec. there was an explosion. U-481 went up to periscope depth and Andersen saw a boat sinking to the right side and the second, probably with a propeller screw damaged by detonation, slowly moving around, unable to manoeuvre. The formation moved east in disorder. Several small, fast boats dispersed in various directions, dropping nine depth charges at irregular intervals. An hour and a half later, the U-481 surfaced to more accurately assess the situation and submit a report to the staff of the 9th Sicherungsdivision on the results of the observation. Suddenly, the lookouts detected in the air a formation of about 100 bombers flying eastwards, with an escort of fighters. The U-Boot immediately hid under the water. When she surfaced after 20 minutes, she was immediately attacked by two attack aircraft. She quickly responded with effective fire, keeping the airplanes flying in the distance. After a few minutes (at 20.25) the attackers moved away, but immediately two more machines came and attacked. The crews of all AA guns opened fire, hitting one of the targets, but the two planes flying from both sides managed to drop six 50-kg bombs: three 50 m behind the stern and three in front of the bow - miraculously causing no damage (not counting the minor damage visible on the anti-shrapnel covers of the 3.7 cm guns). None of the courageous AA crew suffered, while the hit plane fell into the water (the airmen - the pilot and the gunner, managed to survive). U-481 dived. Shortly after 21.00, she surfaced again, in order to - as usual in the last days - withdraw

from her sector for a few hours, giving way to friendly minesweepers. On several occasions, planes flying in the distance were noticed. The expected minesweepers did not arrive.

In the morning, on 31 July, U-481 circled the extensive waters of the previous day's combat. Andersen noted: *Numerous pieces of wood can be seen, life jackets, torn bodies, visible traces show the sinking of at least two vessels.* The day passed again on periscope observation.

At that time, the next U-boats were sent to the Narva Bay.

In the evening U-481 surfaced. The visibility was very good and Andersen moved south, deciding to come closer to the shore. In the air there was a large movement of enemy planes flying in the distance. There were bright flashes of artillery and anti-aircraft fire on the ground, especially from the direction of the port of Narva. A heavily attacked force of own minesweepers again did not reach the area guarded by the U-481.

On the mainland the Red Army troops captured the Latvian town of Tukum, located in central Kurland. Thus, reaching the Gulf of Riga, they cut off the Army Group North (German: Heeresgruppe Nord). At the beginning of August, the peace negotiations between the Finns and the Soviets began - concluding on 2 September with an agreement providing for German troops to leave Finland by 15 September (in fact the German 20th Mountain Army after heavy fighting withdrew to Norway only at the end of October). On the night of 1/2 August, the staff of the 9th Sicherungsdivision informed Andersen of the possibility of operating its Ju 87 Stuka dive bombers near the mine barriers and demanded a report when the enemy minesweepers approached them. During the day, Andersen twice watched from a distance of 7 nm the upcoming formations of Soviet minesweepers, which, however, turned back and went east. In the evening, the headquarters of the 9th Sicherungsdivision informed Andersen of the closure of the passage between the barriers in the area of Nargen Island and demanded a report on the planned return course and the current position and movement of the force of enemy boats. Half an hour later, at 21.00, the U-481 surfaced, but when she noticed two circling enemy fighter aircraft, she immediately dived under the water. After an hour and a half, she surfaced again. Fires were visible from Narva's area. Andersen sent a radiogram: *I have an enemy force at 270°, position 59° 34.4 N, 27° 31.0 E. In the same place the enemy attempts to break through and retire.*

On 2 August, Andersen watched a small group of boats returning to the same place twice. On 3 August, nothing special happened. On 4 August, U-481 was replaced by the U-479 (Oblt. Friedrich-Wilhelm Sons) and left for Tallinn. The technical condition of the U-Boot was already bad, she required urgent repairs. Andersen sums up the patrol:

The location of the enemy: teams of enemy minesweepers were advancing to the southeastern part of the barrier, coming from square 118d73. In this place you should expect a later attempt to break the barrier.

At the same time, simultaneously with minesweeper operations, intensive actions of Russian aviation began to take place very strongly during the day and at night (with the exception of 3 August). Short-lived surfacing during the daylight did not cause any detection by the air force. The battery charging method at night is good. Of the enemy aircraft, the most dangerous and the most aggressive are fighter-bombers, all other machines, especially fighters, "pinch" only lightly but often.

Navigation: with good visibility, there are no difficulties if you know the reconnoitred objects, their longitudes and latitudes (not all are marked on the maps). At night, there is no way to accurately determine the position. In bad, stormy weather, you should deliberately turn slightly to the south. Drifting currents small, possible drift with wind.

Location of the mines: in case of bad wind it is especially necessary to move cautiously with the periscope due to floating mines. Amazing how many of them can suddenly appear.

Procedure in the sector: keep the ship at periscope depth (16 m), moving at "slow ahead" speed. Daily power consumption (without major savings) – 2,500 Ah. Daily consumption of carbon dioxide absorbers with a 21-hour stay under the water - 12-16 units with a small addition of oxygen. The best time for charging the battery - between 23.00 and 02.00 hours.

Communications: good reception on short and long waves.

Underwater listening out: bad conditions.

The second patrol

The stay of U-481 in Tallinn lasted until 10 August, when the radio operator received a new order: *Andersen position I, Schunck (U-348, Oblt. Hans-Norbert Schunck) position II in Narva Bay, replace the U-boats operating there. Put to sea today in time to be in designated positions: Andersen at 23.00, Schunck at 24.00 - 9. Sicherungsdivision.* At 17.00 the U-481 left the port in Tallinn to meet the U-679 (Oblt. [R] Friedrich Breckwoldt). Over the next six days, U-481 encountered and fired at drifting sea-mines many times. She observed a large movement of enemy planes with each surfacing, but was not attacked. Andersen noted in his logbook: *In addition, no special events. Schunck reports on several occasions the detection of a submarine passing under the water. It is impossible, because heavy hailstones cause sounds similar to those produced by electric motors. The storm surges in recent days have caused better listening out conditions.*

On 17 August at 02.00, Andersen met Breckwoldt in the designated place, then moved on to the base on the small island of Nuokko, east of Kotka, where he moored early in the morning. The following morning, the radio operator received a new, unexpected order: *Andersen, go to Helsinki, close the log of combat operations, the ship will undergo a planned repair in Gdynia. Dioxide absorbers and stable food supplies should be donated to Nielsen (U-370, Oblt. Karl Nielsen) - 9. Sicherungsdivision.* Shortly after 14.00 on 18 August, Andersen threw mooring lines in the southern port of Helsinki and reported to the headquarters of the 9th Sicherungsdivision, from where he got acquainted with the current situation: last night (17/18 August) the anti-submarine net called "Sea Urchin" was guarded only by large torpedo boats (with a displacement of 1,294 t , Type 39). They moved at high speed (28 knots) across the Gulf of Finland, along the Kotka - Narva Bay line, ie along the mine barrier. Three of them sank in the barrier: T 22, T 30 and T 32, 393 men perished, only T 23 returned. Only the T 30 had (very little) experience navigating in these waters.

On 19 August, before evening, the U-481 left Helsinki, setting course to Lipau and Konigsberg. On the way, she had to flee under water when she was attacked by two German FW 200 long-range aircraft, not responding to identification signals. Finally, the U-481 was directed to the U-boat base of the 32nd U-Boot Training Flotilla in Konigsberg, where she moored on 21 August at the end of her second patrol.

At that time (20 August), a German force consisting of the heavy cruiser "Prinz Eugen", four destroyers and two torpedo ships in the Gulf of Riga created and maintained the only narrow connection with the cut off troops of Army Group North. At the end of September, the Germans began setting up the mine barrier "Nashorn" ("Rhinoceros") blockading the entrance to the Gulf of Finland between the island of Osmussaar and Finnish port of Hanko.

After almost a month of repair work and loading supplies, the U-481 was again ready for action.

The third patrol

On 15 September, the Red Army broke through the front in the area of Narva, two days later the Kriegsmarine ships were chased off the area of the "Sea Urchin" barrier, while on 21 September the Germans were driven out of Tallinn and Estonia as well as Finland.

In these circumstances, on 19 September, the U-481 began her third patrol. Returning to

All U-Boots were trained in the Gulf of Gdańsk before setting off to perform combat missions, often mooring at the harbour of Danzig.

the Gulf of Finland, she moved from Konigsberg to Libau, where Andersen reported to the headquarters of the U-boats in the Gulf of Finland – the post was recently taken over by a veteran who had commanded three U-boats in the Mediterranean Sea, Korv. Kapt. Albrecht Brandi. After a short briefing, Andersen set off, setting a course to Tallinn, entering the port two days before the Red Army entered it. On these days (21 September), U-242 and U-1001 were laying mines at the Porkkala Peninsula. On 24 September the operational area of U-481 was the sector between the Estonian port of Paldiski (Ger. - Baltisch Port), approximately 30 nm west of Tallinn and Estonian island of Osmussar located approximately 20 nm further westward.

On 10 October, the troops of the Red Army encircled approximately 32 German divisions, about half a million troops of the Army Group North in Kurland, in the region of Libau and Riga. On 15 October, Andersen sank three Finnish sailing craft going from Hanko to Estonia, because he supposed, they were carrying supplies for the Soviets. Their crews were saved.

On 20 October, he decided to enter the bay of the Paldiski harbour in search of targets. He only found two patrol boats anchored there. A torpedo fired from a long distance proved inaccurate.

On the night of 23 October, the U-481 detected a small Soviet convoy sailing slowly from Osmussaar, heading north-east towards Tallinn, staying close to the coast. The night was clear, but not enough for an underwater attack to be effective, so Andersen decided to carry out a surface attack - the only one in U-481's combat record. He surfaced the U-Boot and moved at low speed so as not to reveal the presence of large bow waves, going to a position favourable for the shot. Having a convoy in front of him on the right side at a sharp angle, with targets overlapping, he fired three torpedoes in an arc. However, to the disappointment of the crew, there was not even one detonation, despite the implementation of appropriate torpedo settings. The torpedoes came from old supply stock, which could have caused them to operate improperly. In the face of such a problem, the decision was made to return and two days later, the U-Boot arrived in Danzig, completing the third patrol (after the Germans lost the ports of the Gulf of Finland, the U-boats operated from bases in Danzig and Gdynia).

The fourth patrol

Within a few days U-481 exchanged the old torpedoes, replenished ammunition and food supplies and on 3 November returned to the Osmussaar area. At that time, about 20 Soviet submarines operated successfully in the Gulf of Finland, trying to break into the Baltic Sea, using the help of Finnish minesweepers and pilot boats. The U-481 was able to sense the presence of enemy submarines, even once the sounds of ballasting were clearly heard. After nearly every surfacing, there was an attack by the Soviet aviation, but each time it was effectively repelled and did not pose a great threat to the U-Boot. One dark, foggy night, when the U-481 was on the surface, suddenly, at a distance of only 150 meters, a fast-moving group of Soviet torpedo boats passed by, like a ghost disappearing after

20 seconds, before any response could be made in any way.

On 18 November, the Soviets began an offensive on the island of Saaremaa, separating the Gulf of Riga. On 19 November, the U-481 fired a torpedo at an encountered lighter. Despite a list, she remained on the water, so she was sunk by an anti-aircraft gun. On 28 November, with exceptionally poor conditions for underwater listening out, the largest of the enemy ships encountered so far in the Gulf of Finland was suddenly sighted through the periscope, sailing along a transverse course. Andersen mistakenly took her for the Finnish minelayer "Louhi" (it could have been confusing due to a low, modernised, wide funnel). In fact, it was a Soviet destroyer. Andersen quickly fired a T5 acoustic torpedo (*Zaunkönig* - wren, a homing torpedo intended to be used against the destroyers and other escorts) from the aft tube, scoring a hit. The detonation force also damaged a patrol boat steaming in the immediate vicinity of the ship, which lost its steerability - later it was finished off by the fire of an anti-aircraft gun.

On 12 December, at the entrance to the Gulf of Finland, the expansion of the "Nashorn" mine barrier, which had been laid since September, was performed by a team of three destroyers and two torpedo ships. Two destroyers hit own mines (Z 35 and Z 36). The U-481 and two other U-boats were sent to secure this area from the Finnish coast. The U-481 had a damaged echo sounder, which was a major navigational problem in shallow, coastal waters. Therefore, it was decided to take a working part of it from the U-958, which in the next few days should return to the Gulf of Gdańsk. Both U-boats met at dusk, in a strong wind. There was an accident: the raft returning from the U-958 with the radio operator and two other submariners capsized. Sailors from the U-481 immediately began to search the water, in the dark, using a searchlight - regardless of the danger of their presence being detected. Unfortunately, the search did not work and the U-481 was forced to leave the area. Only one of the missing, a radioman, was taken out several hours later by a fishing boat. In the area of the Finnish side of the "Nashorn" barrier, nothing special happened.

In addition to the U-481 in December, in the Gulf of Finland there were operating: U-475, U-958, U-479, U-679 and U-1165. Andersen was ordered to perform an extremely dangerous task:

Pass underwater through a gap in the "Nashorn" mine barrier, laid in May 1942 (between the Estonian Nargen Island and the Finnish Porkkala Peninsula) to check if it is possible to cross the "Walross" ("Walrus") anti-submarine net located on the eastern side this barrier.

While being on the east side of the net, observe how big is the traffic of Russian convoys between Tallinn and Kronstadt.

Moving near the bottom of the sea, carefully, at the lowest speed called creeping, the U-481 passed under the gap in the mine barrier. At a safe distance from the mines, she surfaced and moved towards the net. It turned out that it could be easily penetrated in many places. The U-Boot returned to the western side of the mine barrier the same way, and Andersen immediately transmitted his observations on the radio.

Six weeks stay at sea had passed, food, fuel and ammunition supplies were low, so the U-481 was ordered to return. On 19 December, she briefly entered the base in Libau, three days later she moored in Danzig, thus ending the patrol.

Late war actions

After a week of waiting, after Christmas the U-Boot underwent a planned month-long renovation in Königsberg. The crew were allowed to take their leaves in two shifts.

On 23 January 1945, Red Army troops occupied Klaipėda (Ger. - Memel), two days later they approached to 15 km from Königsberg, where the fighting intensified. Andersen, who was on leave, was telegraphically called to return immediately. On 27 January, a few hours after his arrival on board of U-481, with another U-boat on tow with broken-down propulsion system, in the evacuation chaos prevailing in the port, left the base in Königsberg, taking a course to Hel. In the Gulf of Gdańsk, there was bad, stormy weather and the voyage was taking place slowly. There was a strong north-easterly wind with a strength of 7-8°. The crew breathed out only in the evening, entering the U-boat base in Hel. Later that evening U-481 set out on her way to Kiel.

A few hours later (after midnight) the senior helmsman performing duty as the 2nd watch officer on the bridge, saw a white light in his sector of observation of the horizon (front right quarter), gradually approaching. Assuming that this was the aft light of a vessel, the II W.O. ordered a left turn to start an overtaking manoeuvre. Suddenly, a second light appeared from the front! It turned out that these were two ships and both sailing straight toward the U-Boot, being close, in a perfect position for ramming! The II W.O. immediately gave the right orders: - *Port side! - Both engines full ahead! - Skipper to the bridge! - Abandon ship!* (the last order meant putting on life jackets and going out on the upper outer deck).

The ship coming from the opposite direction, was - as it turned out - another U-boat, at the last moment it also made a left turn and both ships only lightly collided with their broadsides. After checking the damage, both U-boats together went to the base in Hel, in order to assess the damage in daylight, which turned out to be minor. On 29 January Konigsberg was cut off.

On 30 January, the U-481 set off from Hel, heading west to Kiel. Shortly before midnight, the radio operator received a report on Soviet torpedoes having hit and sunk a passenger ship, transformed into a base for U-Boats, the "Wilhelm Gustloff", with more than 10,000 people aboard. The U-481 was over 100 miles further to the west and could not help. On 1 February the U-Boot entered the base in Kiel, where the ship was to be repaired and the time-consuming procedure of exchanging the snorkels was to be carried out (the old-type valve head of the snorkel device caused flooding by waves, and at the same time created a danger for the crew under pressure inside the rigid hull by working diesels – in the new type of snorkel this problem was eliminated).

On 1 April, the day after the seizure of Danzig by Red Army troops, when the Americans and British crossed the Rhine, Andersen received the order: *Go with two other U-boats to the north, to the Oslofjord, to the U-Boat base in Horten and complete the trials there. After combat readiness is achieved, go along the Norwegian coast to the base of the 14. U-Boot Flotilla in Narvik. Expect operations in the North Sea* (at the time operations in the North Sea were directed by a veteran officer, earlier commanding U-564 with over 125 thousand tons of ships sunk, Freg. Kapt. Reinhard Suhren). In the Kattegat Strait at night there was a strong threat from British aircraft, but radar radiation detector performed well, effectively warning against danger. In order to avoid being detected by the radar of the aircraft, the U-481 remained very close to the Swedish shore (the coastline buildings and structures cause numerous, various, confusing reflections of radar radiation).

On 5 April the crew finished the tests of the new snorkel and the U-Boot sailed along the Norwegian coast to Narvik. At night, she was surprised on the surface by a low-flying plane with a searchlight, but she managed to hide between the rocks so as not to leave a trace on the water. After ten days journey, the U-481 reached Narvik. The crew noticed with astonishment the neglecting of the threat from the air by other U-boats, and even the lack of anti-aircraft gun crews on the surfaced submarines - which was the basis of U-481's safety in the Gulf of Finland.

The last patrol

On 17 April, when one of the last battles of this war was in full swing - the battle for Berlin – the U-481 set out on her last patrol, with the task of attacking west of Bear Island, along with five other U-boats forming a wolf pack called "Faust" ("Fist"), the 22-vessel JW-66 convoy from the Scottish port of the Clyde, which was heavily protected (including an aircraft carrier). After two

days, Andersen took position north of the North Cape. Soon he encountered and sank an unidentified small boat (a fishing boat or small patrol boat). Up to 21 April, German air reconnaissance did not detect the convoy.

The other U-boats had no contact either. The U-481 went down to a depth of 180 m in order to listen out, when a large leak in the combat periscope was revealed, putting it out of use. At periscope depth, they could use only the observation periscope, lower by three meters, so that the air inlet valve of the snorkel protruded more than three meters above the water! The convoy remained undetected, hence Andersen was directed to the area of the entry to the Kola Bay (entrance to Murmansk), in order to attack another convoy going out from there. The submerged U-boot, moving on the snorkel with the protruding mast, was detected and surprised with depth charges dropped by a Sunderland flying boat, forcing Andersen to surface and take up the fight. Accurate fire from the German anti-aircraft guns quickly chased off the plane. From now on, the mast of the snorkel was tilted by 45° to compensate for its height with the periscope (this precautionary method was only safe when the sea was calm and the speed was reduced). Within a few days, Soviet vessels were detected from a distance, but no closer contact was possible. The conditions for keeping watch were very bad. It was not until 29 April, when suddenly the loud sound of the propellers of a destroyer moving at high speed directly towards the U-Boot was heard. Assuming that this was the vanguard of the convoy, Andersen decided to leave the prepared bow torpedo tubes and turn the ship to launch a T 5 homing torpedo from the stern tube at close range. Probably the fast-approaching destroyer noticed the head of the observation periscope (much larger than the head of the immobilized combat periscope). The torpedo was fired almost at the last minute, but it was not accurate. The U-Boot went deeper at the highest possible speed. At a depth of 25 m, the first depth charges exploded in close proximity, causing numerous damages to the electrical system. The ship dropped down quickly. It was only at a depth of 220 m that the descent was stopped. The rigid hull was, thankfully, watertight. There was silence, and then the sounds of propellers appeared over the submarine. Suddenly, there was a very powerful explosion, causing numerous other failures, but no leaks. After several minutes, the sound of propellers began to fade, the destroyer went away. The state of the U-Boot's devices was checked and the ship went up to periscope depth. For the next long hours, the diesel work on the snorkel would have to be very limited, the supply of compressed air was low and it was necessary to save it. So Andersen waited until midnight until complete darkness came and

ter was damaged, but the receiver worked. In the following days, the crew learned from the radio about Hitler's suicide and the fall of Berlin. On 3 May the U-481 arrived in the Kilbotn U-boat base near Harstadt, mooring at an ex-Norwegian passenger vessel, now the base ship "Black Watch". Later that same evening Andersen sailed out of the base, wanting to be in Narvik the next day. In the morning, the radio operator received news of the sinking of the "Black Watch" by British bomber aircraft, together with a U-boat and tanker moored to her, as well as the bombing of the shipyard in Narvik. Many Germans were killed. On 4 May, the U-481 was moored at a small, makeshift shipyard in Bogen, in Ofotfjord. The technical condition of the U-Boot was disastrous: the submersion system required renewing, both periscopes needed to be replaced. News from the front was also depressing for the Germans. Shortly after analysing the situation and receiving the order to cease hostilities, Andersen joined 12 other U-boats, whose commanders decided to move from Narvik to Trondheim, which seemed a much safer place. On the way, at the western exit from the fjord, they were stopped by the British 9th Escort Group.

On 17 May, the U-boot commanders received their last radio orders: *06.03 hours: U-278, 313, 992, 968, 997, 716, 318, 295, 363, 668, 312, 427, 294, 2526, 481.*

All U-Boots will be led by corvettes to Scotland.

Command of the U-boots is taken over by Kptlt. Franze (commanding officer of U-278).

No U-Boot must be destroyed or sunk.

Move in two columns 750 m apart, distance 400 m, course 270°, speed 10 kn. Order in columns as before.

Signalling between each other is forbidden. Commands are received and forwarded by Franze.

Franze, mark the ship with a yellow flag.
Commanding officer of the U-Boots.
Time 06.57:
The U-boots in the North Sea. Regretfully, I release you from service. I trust in your discipline. You were faithful, tough, with your eyes wide open. See you in the homeland. Your Commander.

Time 07.12

The U-Boots in the North Sea. I am passing you my best wishes. Thank you for your faithfulness. See you later. Your Commander.

First, the U-Boots entered Eriboll for a short time, then they moved to Loch Alsh, where more than half of the crews were disembarked, and eventually docked in Londonderry.

On 30 November 1945 at 10.09, the U-481 went down, sunk by gunfire as part of Operation "Deadlight", 120 nm west of the Scottish coast.

SOURCE: KTB U-481 AND PHOTOS: DEUTSCHE U-BOOT-
MUSEUM IN CUXHAVEN

In the second half of 1943, U-Boots received new, very effective, twin- and quadruple- barrel, 2 cm anti-aircraft guns.

the ship surfaced dynamically, coming to the surface at high speed without blowing the tanks. Immediately after the conning tower surfaced and the horizon was checked by the watch officer, the drive was switched from electric to diesel (which worked without a problem) and the ballast tanks were slowly blown out with exhaust fumes. The diesels worked well. It seemed that the danger had passed when the effects of close detonations of depth charges were noticed: torn wooden elements along the entire length of the upper deck, bridge housing and railings bent, rubber boats' lockers opened, and a wide oil trail behind the U-Boot. The floating remains must have been the evidence of sinking the U-boot for the destroyer skipper, which was why he quickly sailed away. Andersen decided to return to base on the surface and to stay close to the coast. The transmit-

Magazines

Books

Events

Kagero Publishing was found in year 1995. It is specialising in releasing historic and military books and magazines – being one of their biggest distributors on Polish and foreign market. Kagero Publishing is a well known organizer of educational patriotic events promoting Polish aviation traditions in Lublin province. It is the originator and producer of International Air Picnic **LOTNICZE DEPUŁTYCZE** which two editions were very popular within local and country wide audience.

Photos: Kagero Archive, Albert Osiński

kagero.eu
eventylotnicze.eu

KAGERO Publishing
ul. Akacjowa 100,
Turka, os. Borek,
20-258 Lublin 62, Poland

Italian Battleships In Drawings

Witold Koszela

The "Conte di Cavour" seen from a deck of another vessel.

The "Conte di Cavour's" guns.

On the eve of the outbreak of World War Two, the Italian Regia Marina was one of the world's foremost war fleets, with many ships of considerable combat value.

Cruisers classified as heavy and light, destroyers and submarines constituted a significant part of it, but the true determinant of the power of a given fleet of that period were the battleships, and here the Italians could boast of extremely interesting vessels with significant combat value and unusual design. Trying to implement the strategy of controlling the central part of the Mediterranean Sea and, of course, considering the disarmament treaties, they kept in service two types of battleships built during the First World War – the Cavour class: "Conte di Cavour" and "Giulio Cesare" and Andrea Doria class: „Andrea Doria" and „Caio Duilio". They were extraordinary ships.

Although it might seem that these ships - built after all in completely different times - did not have great combat values, all four had undergone large-scale refurbishment, almost completely changing their specifications and appearance.

They were supplemented with three, or actually four, modern Vittorio Veneto class (also known as Littorio class) named: "Vittorio Veneto", "Littorio" (the name was later changed to "Italia"), "Roma" and "Impero".

It cannot be denied that in June 1940, when under the leadership of Benito Mussolini, Italy joined the war as an ally of the Third Reich, the Regia Marina was a power that posed a huge threat to the Allied forces in the Mediterranean.

Interestingly, at that time their navy, which in terms of war readiness was the best in comparison with the ground forces and aviation, had only two fully operational battleships: "Conte di Cavour" and "Giulio Cesare", which relatively recently had their passed an upgrade programme and could now carry out combat tasks. Shipyard work on the "Duilio" came to an end in the summer of 1940, and on "Andrea Doria" in the autumn of the same year.

The situation was similar with the Vittorio Veneto class vessels, of which the first two battleships - "Vittorio Veneto" and "Littorio" - were already launched and entered service in April and May 1940, but it must be remembered that there was still a long time needed for them to conduct appropriate training. The worst situation was in case of the third of the battleship series - "Roma" - which entered service only in June 1942, and the fourth ship of this type - "Impero" - which was launched in November 1939, never entered service.

One kind of curiosity is the widely prevailing opinion that the Italian's major ships, including battleships, were led to the fight very rarely, and if they participated in the battle, they were on the losing side. But having analysed their history, it is easy to see that it was not exactly like that, as can be demonstrated by a number of interesting operations.

The British were also well aware of the power of Italian battleships, often dodging the fight when they went out to sea and carrying out attacks on Italian bases and ships stationed in them.

The fate of Italian battleships went differently and in many cases their stories looked very interesting, but their detailed description is a topic for another study. This article will focus on the profiles of these ships, which, as you can see, were unusual. In various references you can often find an opinion in which the authors consider them to be some of the most beautiful ships of the World War Two period, writing about their harmonious shapes, design and interesting camouflage patterns.

SOURCE OF PHOTOS: ARCHIVE OF THE AJ-PRESS PUBLISHING HOUSE AND AUTHOR'S COLLECTIONS

The "Giulio Cesare" aftes she had been refurbished.

The "Littorio" during the sea trials.

Built at the Cantieri Ansaldo shipyard in Genoa, the "Giulio Cesare" entered service in May 1914. At that time, the ship had 24,800 t full displacement, measured 176.09 m total length, beam 28 m and had a total output of 31,000 HP (a maximum speed of 22 knots). It was armed with 13 305 mm guns, 18 120 mm guns, 13-14 76 mm guns, and 3 450 mm torpedo tubes.

In 1933-1937, at the Cantieri Navali del Tirreno e Riuniti shipyard in Genoa, the "Giulio Cesare" had undergone major modernization, after which she gained a lot, becoming a ship with modern armament, a new power unit and a much more attractive silhouette.

Drawings
Witold Koszela

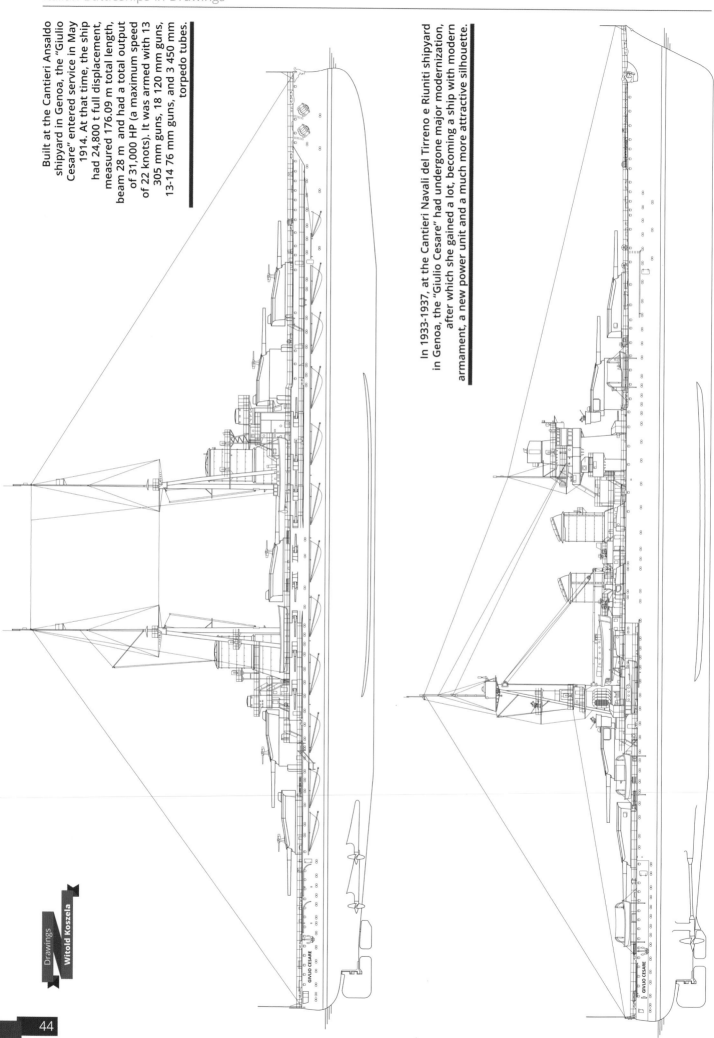

GIULIO CESARE

GIULIO CESARE

Commissioned in 1915, the "Conte di Cavour", like her sister ship "Giulio Cesare", in the mid-1930s underwent a large-scale modernization, which altered her characteristics and profile to the requirements of the then modern marine warfare. At that time, the ship had 29,100 t full displacement, was 186.4 m in total length, beam of 28 m and a maximum speed of 27 knots. The armament consisted of 10 320 mm guns, 12 120 mm guns, 8 100 mm guns, 12 37 mm and 12 13.2 mm anti-aircraft guns.

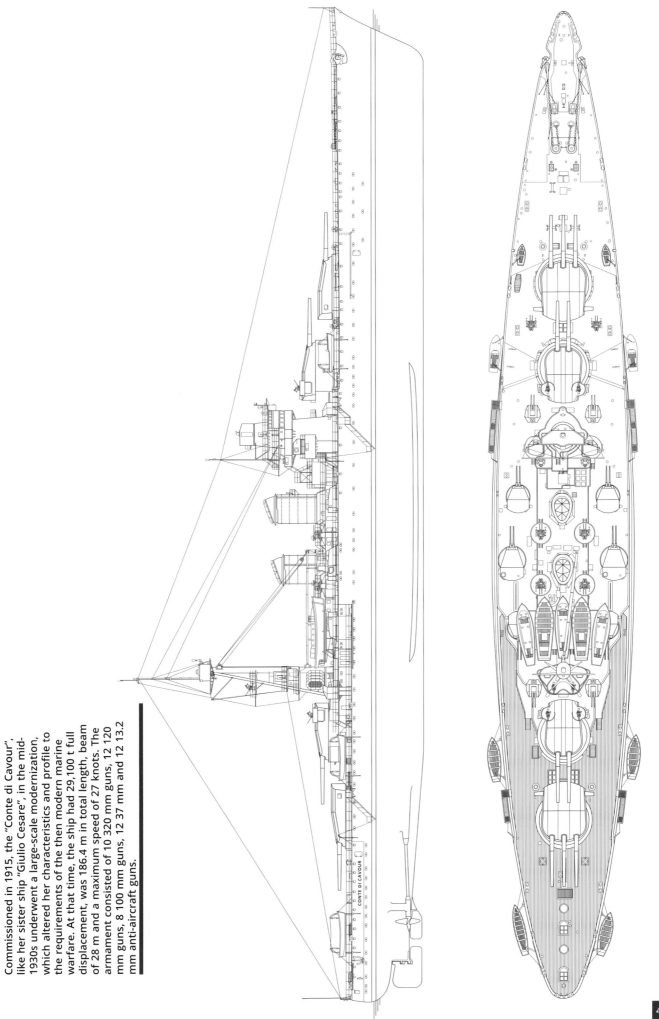

CONTE DI CAVOUR

Drawings
Witold Koszela

"Conte di Cavour" in colour. The elegance of this ship could not be denied.

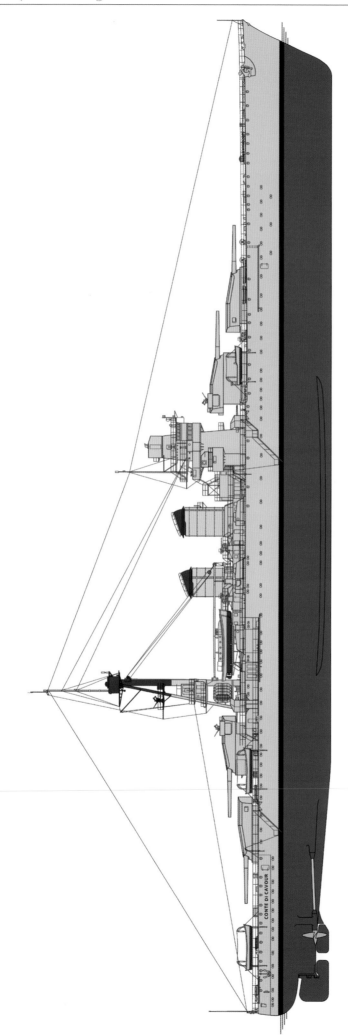

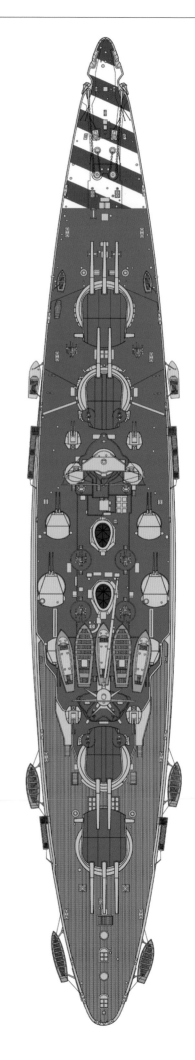

CONTE DI CAVOUR

Introduced in 1915, "Caio Duilio" was built at the Cantieri di Castellammare di Stabia shipyard. The ship had at that time 25,200 t full displacement, measured 176.1 m in overall length, beam 28 m and a maximum speed of 21.5 knots. The armament consisted of 13 305 mm guns, 16 152 mm guns, 13 76 mm guns, 2 40 mm guns and 2 450 mm torpedo tubes.

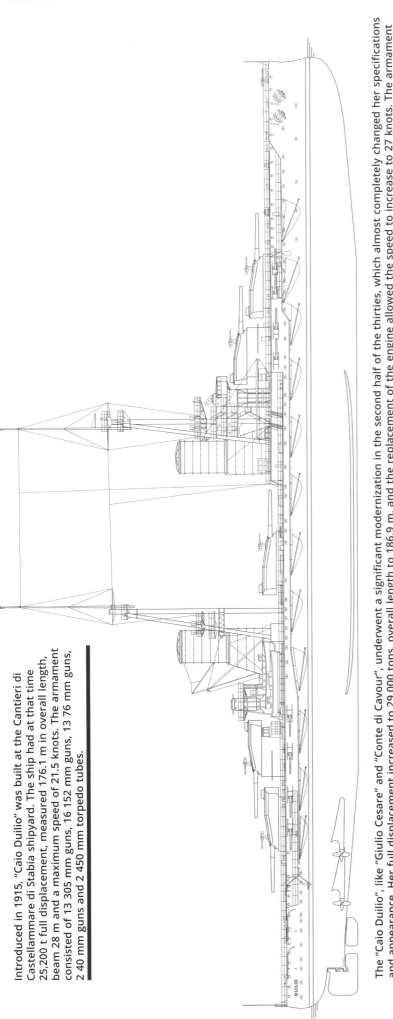

The "Caio Duilio", like "Giulio Cesare" and "Conte di Cavour", underwent a significant modernization in the second half of the thirties, which almost completely changed her specifications and appearance. Her full displacement increased to 29,000 tons, overall length to 186,9 m, and the replacement of the engine allowed the speed to increase to 27 knots. The armament consisted of 10 320 mm guns, 12 135 mm guns, 10 90 mm guns, 19 37 mm guns and 12 20 mm cannons.

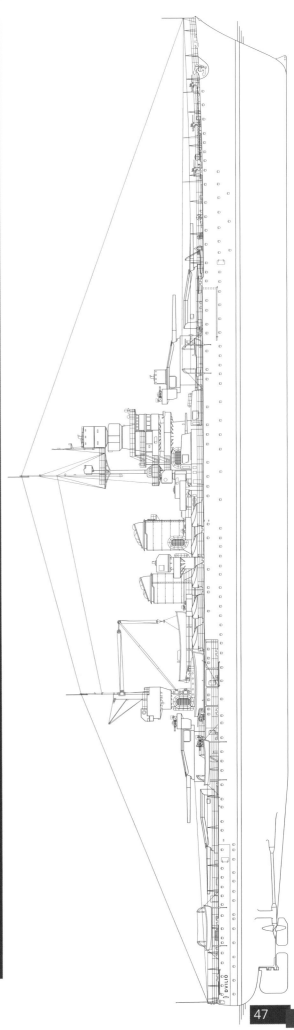

Drawings
Witold Koszela

The "Caio Duilio" sporting a camouflage pattern applied from 1941.

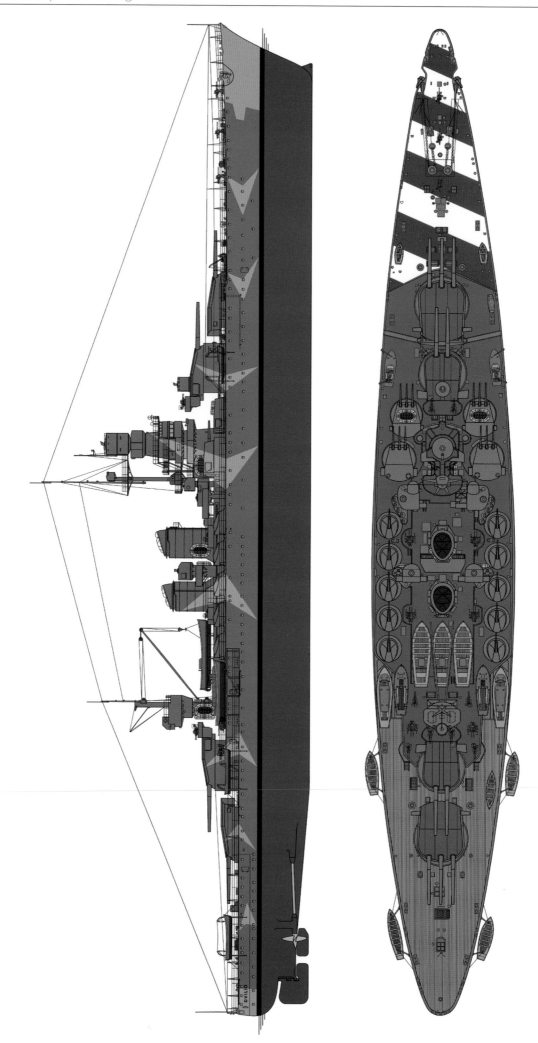

The "Andrea Doria" was built at the Arsenale di La Spezia shipyard and entered service in 1916. Like her sister ship, "Caio Duilio", she underwent extensive modernization thanks to which she became a ship with significant combat value. In 1940, her full displacement amounted to 29,000 t, overall length 186.9 m, beam 28 m, and with engine room output of 85,000 hp she could speed at 27 knots. She was armed with 10 320 mm guns, 12 135 mm guns, 10 90 mm guns, 19 37 mm guns and 12 20 mm cannons.

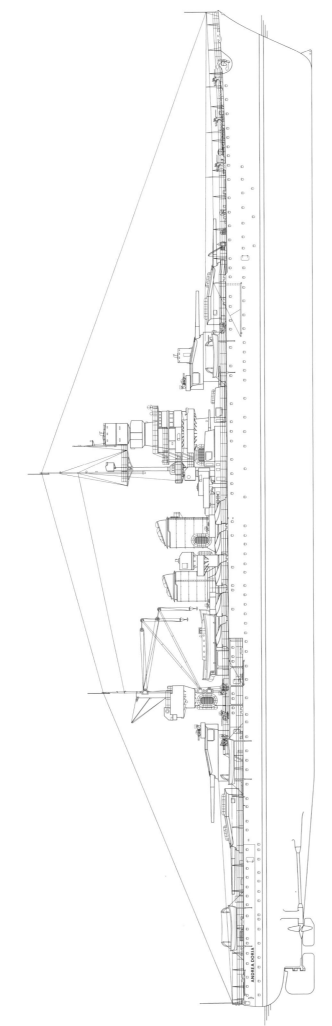

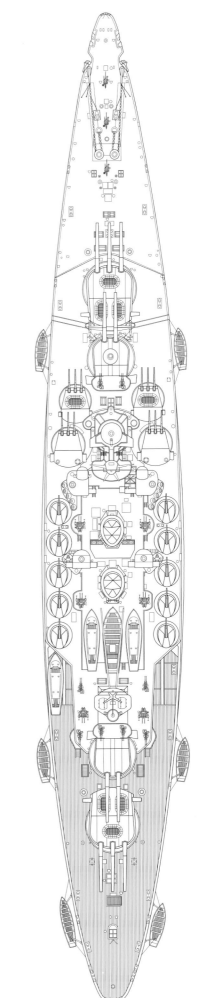

The "Vittorio Veneto" opened a new chapter in the history of Italian shipbuilding. Built at the Cantieri Riuniti dell'Adriatico shipyard in Trieste, she was one of the best in her class. Her full displacement was 45,750 tons, overall length was 237.7 m, beam was 32.9 m, and speed at an output of 134,600 HP was 31.4 knots. She was armed with 9 381 mm guns, 12 152 mm guns, 12 90 mm guns, 19 37 mm guns and 32 20 mm cannons.

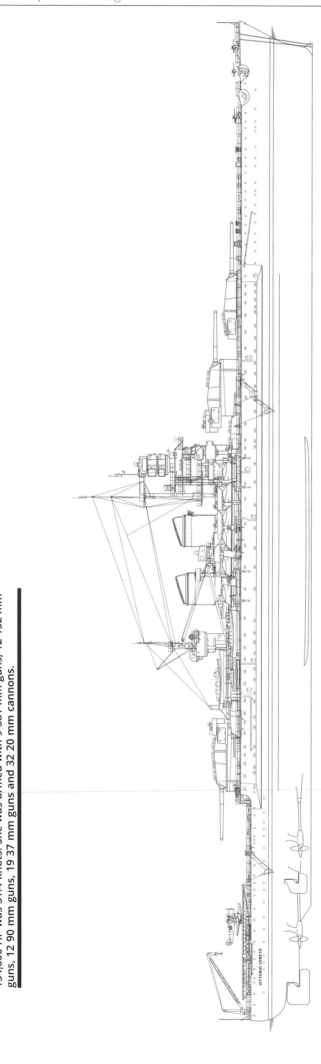

VITTORIO VENETO

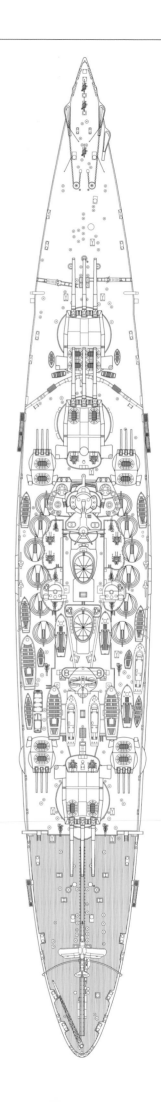

Introduced in May 1940, "Littorio" was built at the Cantieri Ansaldo shipyard in Genoa. The ship had 45,960 t full displacement, length 237.7 m, beam 32.9 m, and the output of her engines reached 139,560 HP, which allowed the development of a maximum speed of 31.2 knots. Her armament was made up of 9 381 mm gun, 12 152 mm guns, 12 90 mm guns, 20 37 mm guns and 24 20 mm cannons. In July 1943 she was re-named "Italia".

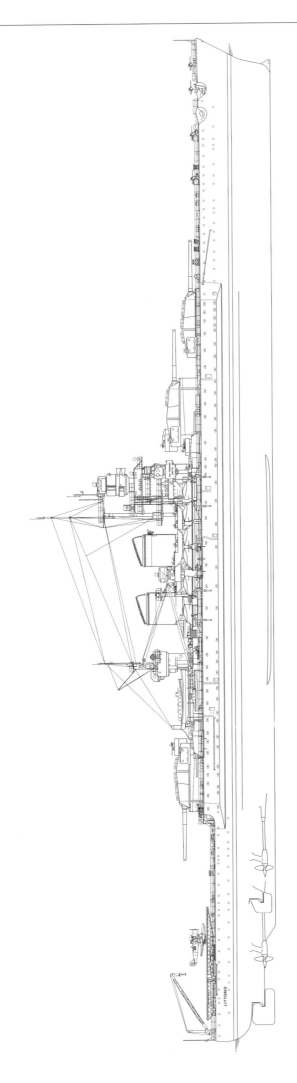

The "Littorio" in the standard camouflage pattern from the initial period of service. The painting scheme of all Italian line ships of World War Two was characterized by diagonal white and red stripes at the bow and stern (later only at the bow), which were the result of problems by Italian pilots with the identification of their own ships.

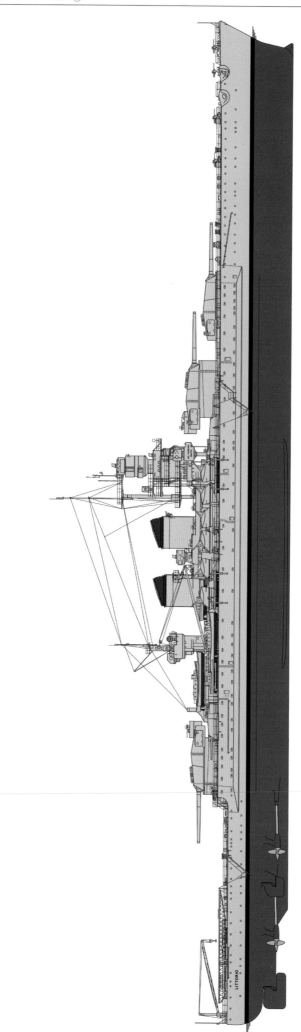

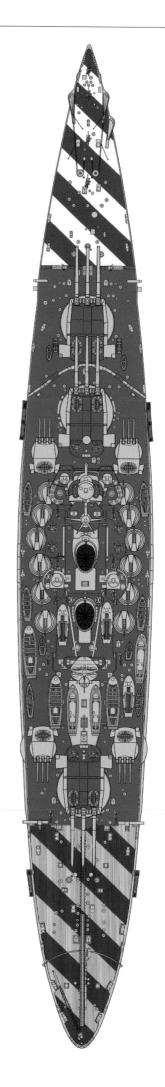

Introduced into service as the last, in June 1942, the battleship "Roma" was built at Cantieri Riuniti dell'Adriatico in Trieste. The ship was slightly different from her sister ships "Vittorio Veneto" and "Littorio". She had 46,200 t full displacement, 238.8 m overall length and beam 32.9 m. Her engines reached an output of 130,000 hp, thanks to which she achieved a speed of 29 knots. She was armed with 9 381 mm guns, 12 152 mm guns, 12 90 mm guns, 20 37 mm guns and 32 20 mm cannons.

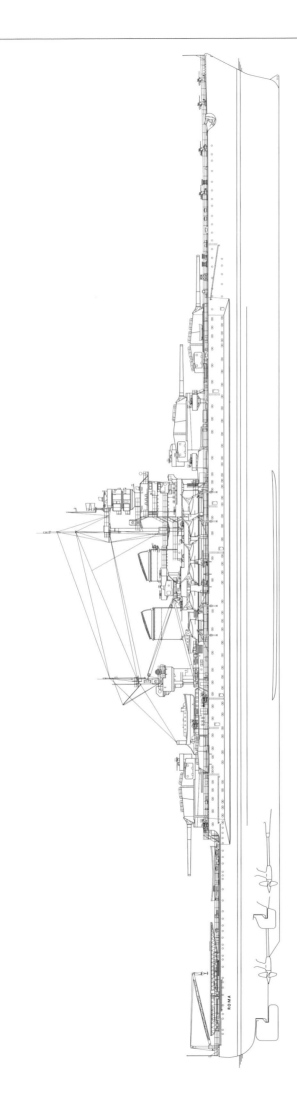

Drawings
Witold Koszela

The "Roma" in camouflage pattern she sported in 1943.

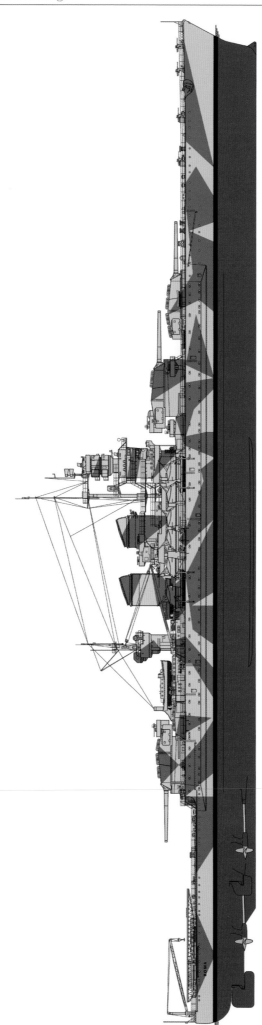

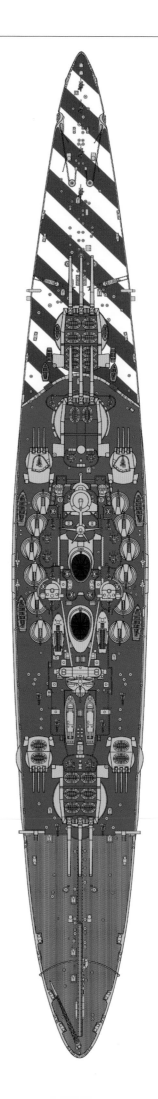

The arrangement of decks as seen on the modernized battleship "Giulio Cesare".

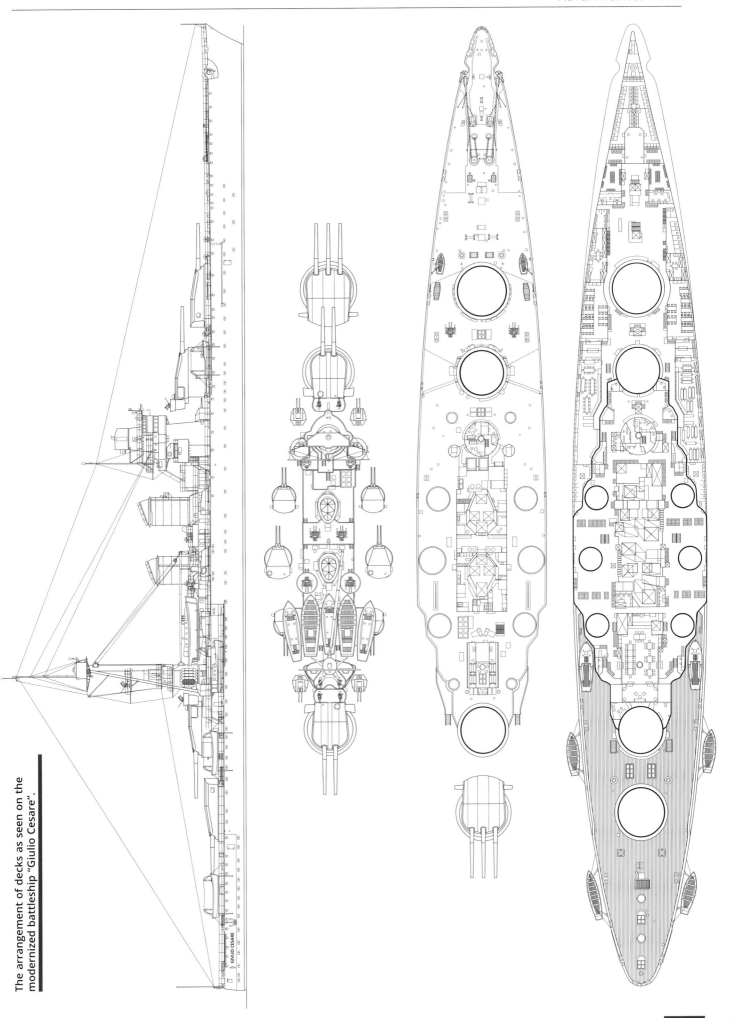

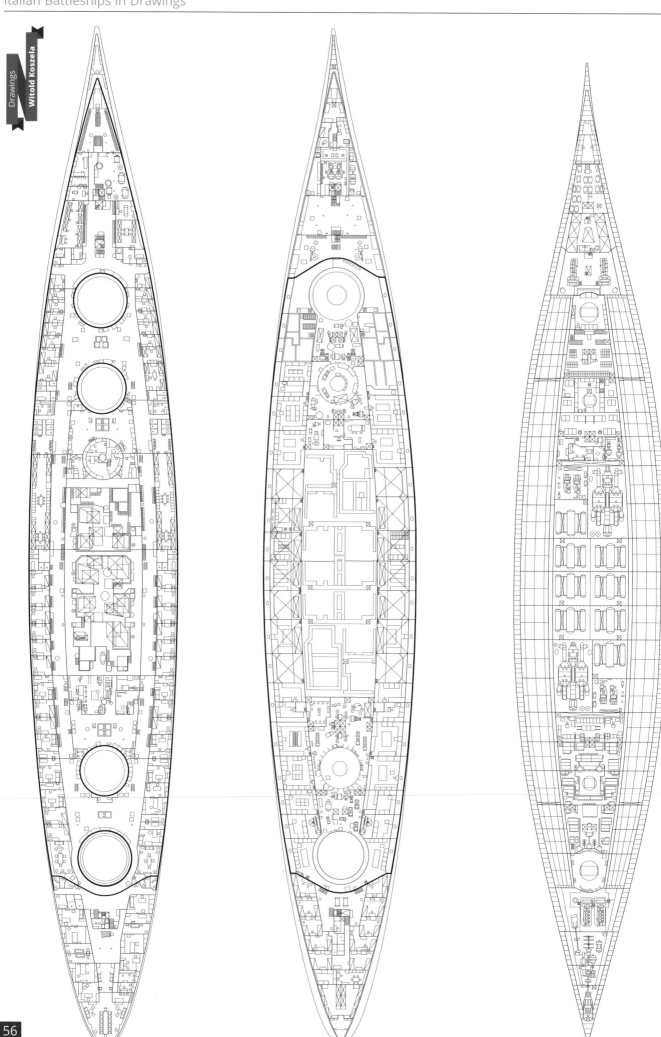

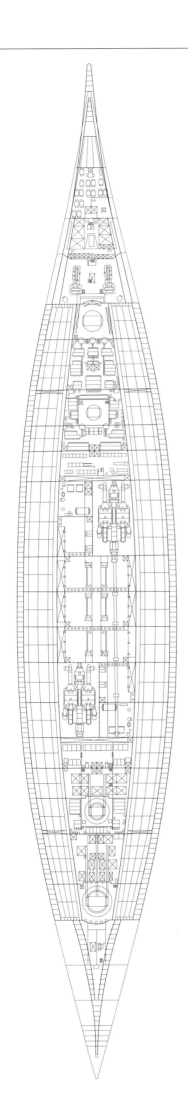
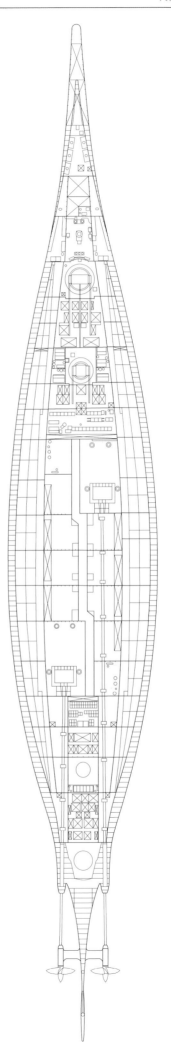

Lemoore Prepares For Lightning Strike!

Patrick Roegies, Paul Gross, Hans Looijmans

The U.S. Navy aircraft carrier USS "Carl Vinson" (CVN-70) transits the Pacific Ocean on 31 May 2015. "Carl Vinson" and its embarked air wing, Carrier Air Wing 17 (CVW-17), were in the U.S. 3rd Fleet area of operations returning to homeport after a deployment to the U.S. 5th and 7th Fleets. [Internet]

Introduction

Currently the Navy has stationed its F/A-18 Hornet fleet at two Strike Fighter Super Hornet/Hornet bases. NAS Oceana on the East Coast and NAS Lemoore on the West Coast.

As of 2012 the mid-term plan included the relocation of two East Coast squadrons to the West Coast. This relocation was deemed necessary in order to provide the strike fighter community fighter squadrons to meet the changing operational demand in the Pacific. It also enables the Navy to mitigate a possible shortage in strike fighter community assets due to the aging FA-18 "Legacy Hornet" aircraft. Conversion of up to

an additional five Strike Fighter squadrons from "Legacy Hornet" to "Super Hornet" squadrons should result in the alignment of Strike Fighter community assets to meet carrier air wing deployment schedules, and to ensure sufficient Strike Fighter capability is present in the short term.

Current conversion to Super Hornet

The conversion of F/A-18 squadrons at NAS Lemoore to Super Hornet squadrons is in full progress. In 2014 both VFA-97 " Warhawks" and VFA-192 "Golden Dragons" were in the process of conversion. VFA-97's conversion to Super Hornets commenced in December 2013. The last "Warhawk"

Legacy Hornets left NAS Lemoore in November 2013 and the first Super Hornets arrived at the squadron on December 2nd 2013. VFA-97 took delivery of brand new factory delivered F/A-18E's. Carrier deck qualifications took place in February 2014 on the USS "George Bush" and were completed successfully.

VFA-192 received their first Super Hornets by the end of 2013 but in contrast to VFA-97 they did not receive factory new F/A-18E's. Instead of receiving brand new factory Hornets the squadron received Lot 23/24 FA-18E Super Hornets which were acquired from VFA-27. Since these Hornets were already appointed to VFA-27 and had already seen considerable action before they were transferred to VFA-192, each aircraft that was received was subjected to thorough maintenance, in practice meaning that the entire airframe was stripped and inspected.

The two remaining squadrons at NAS Lemoore operating the Legacy Hornets are VFA-94 and VFA-113. The intention is to complete the entire conversion by 2015.

For newly winged aviators from the training commands, their next assignment before arriving at an operational squadron is to go to a Fleet Replacement Squadron (FRS) formerly known as and still usually referred to as the RAG squadron (The FRS's were formerly known as *Replacement Air Groups*, and are thus commonly called "Rags"). The appointed FRS squadron at Lemoore is VFA-122. At VFA-122 the fresh aviators will go through an entire syllabus to learn the basics of operating and tactically employing the Hornet or Rhino before they are assigned to an operational squadron. New aviators at the FRS will go through a series of familiarization simulators before their first flight in the F-18. The first few flights are dualed up in a trainer aircraft, but the first solo comes much earlier than in the T-34, T-6 or T-45 syllabus. After that point the 'Cones' as the trainees are affectionately referred to will progress through the syllabus and perform

Prior to their deployment to the USS Carl Vinson the Carrier Air Wing 17 to which VFA-94 is appointed was present at NAS Fallon in April 2014. The "Mighty Shrikes" will receive the aircraft which were appointed to VFA-2 which were traded for new ones.

The VFA-113 CAG bird was captured during the morning launch of CAW-17 deployment to NAS Fallon early April 2014 prior to their embarkation to the USS Carl Vinson. This will be the last cruise of VFA-113 operating the "Legacy" Hornet.

The U.S. Navy aircraft carrier USS "Carl Vinson", 2003. [Internet]

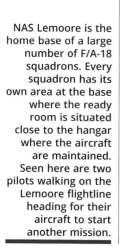

NAS Lemoore is the home base of a large number of F/A-18 squadrons. Every squadron has its own area at the base where the ready room is situated close to the hangar where the aircraft are maintained. Seen here are two pilots walking on the Lemoore flightline heading for their aircraft to start another mission.

various air-to-surface and air-to-air flights, some of which will be conducted as solo aircrew and some with an instructor in the back seat. The RAG students are referred to as "Cones" because new F-18 pilots are considered "Category One" (Cat One - C. One - "Cone") students. There are 4 categories. Cat 1 is brand new students flying the F-18. Cat 2 would be for pilots with tactical jet experience, but transitioning into the F-18 (like the Tomcat, S-3, etc). Cat 3 and 4 are for F-18 pilots that have been out of the cockpit for a certain amount of time.

The operational squadrons are responsible for training up their new aircrew to become section and division flight leads. The weapons school at NAS Fallon mostly trains candidates going through the Top Gun course or provides training to air wings while they're working up for their deployments at NAS Fallon.

Preparing for Lightning Strike!

The Navy's conversion to the F-35C Lightning II is currently in the early stages.

Coupled with the US military realignment strategy NAS Lemoore is to become the largest fighter hub in the US Navy. The plan comprises the relocation of two East Coast Super Hornet squadrons to geographically align and equally divide the strike fighter squadrons with the current Carrier Air Wing deployment requirements. In the current situation two East Coast squadrons are the subject of multiple cross continental transits to train and certify with the aircraft carrier and Carrier Strike Group. Relocating the East Coast Strike Fighter Squadrons to NAS Lemoore would provide neces-

NAS Lemoore uses four H-60 Blackhawks for rescue purposes. Seen here is one of the MH-60S appointed to the Search And Rescue (SAR) detachment.

Most of the MH-60S helicopters have been painted in a with and orange paint scheme. MH-60S appointed BuNo 166339 appointed modex 7S-02 is still painted in a standard navy grey paint.

sary support without duplication of existing home base support functions and would realign the Fleet with East/West operational commitments.

The proposed action would relocate two East Coast FA-18E/F Super Hornet squadrons to NAS Lemoore. The two squadrons that are nominated to be relocated to NAS Lemoore are VFA-11 and VFA-136. Specifically, the proposed Strike Fighter realignment would consist of the following primary actions which already commenced from 2013 forward:

– Two existing squadrons VFA-97 and VFA-151 completed their transition from 10-plane Hornet squadrons to 10-plane Super Hornet

VFA-147 received their first FA-18C Hornets on 6 December 1989. The Argonauts were the FIRST squadron to receive the new Lot XII "Night Attack" Hornets and quickly put them in action on their first WESTPAC deployment to the Persian Gulf in March of 1991. Combat air patrol missions over Iraq and Kuwait in support of Operation Desert Storm during troop withdrawal operations highlighted the deployment. The Argonauts continued spearheading the F/A-18's maturation as the Navy's premiere strike aircraft by being the Navy's FIRST operational night attack squadron to employ Target and Navigational Forward Looking Infra-Red PODS (NAV FLIR) and night vision goggles. In May of 1998 the Argonauts groomed their Lot XVI Hornets for an unusual but highly successful transfer to VFA-195 stationed in Yokosuka, Japan. In return VFA-147 received twelve Lot XI Hornets, and also a new home aboard the USS JOHN C. STENNIS (CVN-74).

In April 2001, VF-14 embarked on their final F-14 cruise on board USS Enterprise (CVN-65), supporting Operation Southern Watch and Operation Enduring Freedom. After their last F-14 cruise VF-14 and VF-41 relocated to NAS Lemoore and began the transition to the F/A-18 Super Hornet switching to CVW-11 and USS Nimitz (CVN-68).

squadrons. The conversion commenced in 2013 and was completed by the end of the year.

– VFA-192 started their transition from a 10-plane Hornet squadron to a 10-plane Super Hornet squadron in 2014 is and was completed that same year.

– VFA-146 started their transition in January 2015 from a 10-plane Hornet squadron to a 12-plane Super Hornet squadron and has recently completed their conversion.

– The two remaining squadrons VFA-113 and VFA94 equipped with the F/A-18C are currently on a deployment on board the USS carl Vinson. Upon their return to NAS Lemoore the squadrons will start their transition to the Super Hornet. VFA-94 will acquire the old VFA-2 F/A-18F's and VFA-113 will receive the F/A-18E. Depending on the return of these two squadrons the conversion process will be started and completed which is planned for 2015.

The aircraft carrier USS "George H.W. Bush" (CVN 77) is underway in the Atlantic Ocean. "George H.W. Bush" is underway conducting a composite training unit exercise. [U.S. Navy photo by Mass Communication Specialist 3rd Class Nicholas Hall/ Released]

VFA-41 traded their F-14A Tomcats for F/A-18F Super Hornets in 2001. With the transfer to the F/A-18F the squadron kept their two person crew in their new aircraft. The commander aircraft carries BuNo166842 and modex NG-100. It was captured at NAS Lemoore at the Black Aces flightline before taxiing out. Due to the 70th Anniversary of the squadron the aircraft has received a new celebration painting.

VFA-25 nicknamed the Fist of the Fleet also reside at NAS Lemoore. In May 1983, pilots from VA-25 began training in the new F/A-18A Hornet. In the fall of 2012 VFA-25 completed it's transition to the F/A-18E Super Hornet, as part of its transition, TWO FIVE joined Carrier Air Wing NINE onboard USS JOHN C. STENNIS (CVN 74).

– Hangars 1, 2 and 4 were modified for the purpose to host the Super Hornets

– Hangars 5 and 6 will be modified to host the new F-35C aircraft

– As a separate action NAS Lemoore would reduce the number of training aircraft in its train-ing squadron VFA-122 between 2012 and 2013 which is already completed.

– Both East Coast Super Hornet squadrons will arrive at NAS Lemoore by 2017. Strike Fighter Squadron VFA-136 will relocate as a 12-plane FA-18E squadron and Strike Fighter Squadron VFA-

VFA-192 Golden dragons completed their transition to the Super Hornet in 2014 receiving the former "VFA-27 aircraft. This were Lot 23/24 aircraft and were completely refurbished by VFA-192 maintenance personnel upon arrival.

The current Fleet Replacement Squadron on the west coast is VFA-122 and is equipped with both Legacy Hornets and Super Hornets and even has one F/A-18A+ Hornet in their inventory.

"George H. W. Bush" (top) conducts an ordnance transfer with "Harry S. Truman" off the East Coast in 2011. [Internet]

During their work up training the Carrier Air Wings transfer to NAS Fallon. Uring their training the crews fly multiple missions against VFC-13 adversary squadron in order to gain experience in air to air combat.

11 as a 12-plane F/A-18F squadron. One squadron is planned to be relocated in June 2016 and the other squadron is planned to relocate in January 2017.

The plans became more specific when the Navy announced that NAF El Centro will not be the host for the US Pacific Fleet F-35C aircraft. In the previous years several studies have been conducted to determine the possibilities, the necessary requirements and the consequences of transferring NAF El Centro into a Homebase for the

Pacific "Lightning" Strike force. Apparently these plans have been abandoned and NAS Lemoore was the remaining alternative to be the host. This means NAS Lemoore is planning for the arrival of the new aircraft with conversion to Super Hornet still in progress.

The intended target is to transfer NAS Lemoore from a host of 15 F/A-18C, E and F squadrons into a base of 17 F-35C and F/A-18E/F squadrons between 2028 and 2030. The "end situation" will count 7 F-35C squadrons, 6 F/A-18F squadrons

Besides the F-5N the Navy uses the F-16 in the adversary roll. These F-16's are appointed to NSAWC and are also based at NAS Fallon.

and 4 F/A-18E squadrons. Each squadron will be equipped with 10 aircraft. When the plan is completed NAS Lemoore will host 60% of the Navy strike fighter capacity within the Navy.

Fleet Replacement preparations

Strike Fighter Squadron VFA-101 is currently based at Eglin Air Force Base being the initial squadron equipped with the F-35C. Initially VFA-101 was an F-14 RAG squadron and used to be based at NAS Oceana. When VFA-101 withdrew the F-14's from use the squadron was appointed

as the Fleet Replacement Squadron (FRS) for the F-35C. The squadron moved to Eglin AFB and is expected to move to its new Homebase NAS Lemoore in January 2017.

VFA-101 is currently in the process of gaining newly delivered aircraft, training instructor pilots and maintainers preparing for their new task at NAS Lemoore. One year after its arrival at NAS Lemoore the squadron will begin to transition fleet squadrons into the F-35C. The conversion process too is expected to take one year to accomplish initially and with more squadron shifts from the Hornet to the Lightning II the

The F-5N's appointed to VFC-13 were acquired from the Swiss Air Force. Upon arrival the F-5's were refurbished and overhauled and currently fulfill the adversary role in order to train the Carrier Air Wing pilots in real time air to air combat missions.

The F-16's appointed to NSAWC are painted in a two tone brown and two tone blue camouflage scheme. The F-16's appointed to NSAWC were originally planned for delivery to the Pakistan Air Force. These aircraft were never actually delivered and as a result were appointed to NSAWC.

NAS Lemoore and the aircraft of VFA-14 before another sortie.

squadron hopes to be more efficient by gained experience and shorten the conversion time. It is intended that VFA-101 will be equipped with 30 aircraft in order to perform its training and conversion mission. If the plan is actually met depends on the pass of delivery of the new F-35C's to the Navy.

The first squadron to transfer to the F-35C is VFA-97 "Warhawks" is planned for January 2018. This might change due to a number of factors such as changes in the deployment schedules and could have an impact on this decision.

The project officer on the staff of Strike Fighter Wing Pacific is Cmdr. Ryan "Spool" Douglas. Already Douglass and planners have started work on the relocation to NAS Lemoore. They will begin by reworking the existing hangar 5. Douglass has planned the military construction over the next 10 years constantly growing F-35 presence on the base. The new hangars will be constructed based on a module concept where each appointed squadron will have their own module intended for 4 squadrons host in the future. The design is currently completed and has been send out to contractor bids. The plan is to start reconstructions of the first module in July 2015. In 2015 the remaining 3 modules are planned to be reconstructed which will take approximately 2 years to complete. Once completed VFA-101 and the first currently selected transition fleet squadron VFA-97 will take up

residence in the hangar. In 2018 constructions are planned to start on hangar 6, to be the host of the other selected F-35C squadrons.

Compared to an F/A-18 squadron an F-35C squadron has an additional number of enlisted maintainers planned. Where an F/A-18E/F squadron counts between 226 and 234 FTE an F-35C squadron is planned to require between 245 and 250 FTE. The main reason is the creation of an entirely new maintenance shop manned by aviation structural mechanics for each F-35C squadron and will be responsible for maintaining the outside of the aircraft. The used skin material of the F-35C has stealth capabilities and is designed to deflect radar. Since the importance of Stealth capability it is important that there will be a new maintenance shop in the squadron, manned by personnel with special training and skills.

PHOTO SOURCE: IF NOT SIGNED DIFFERENTLY, THEN PHOTOS FROM THE AUTHORS' COLLECTIONS

This ex-Swiss J-3025 was delivered to the US Navy in 2008. Currently it is a part of the VFC-13 Squadron "The Saints". We can see it here while taking off to perform another mission in a role of "an aggressor".

The T-34A "Mentor" - the aircraft of this type belong to the VFA-122 and serve as the basic trainers. They would be replaced in the near future.

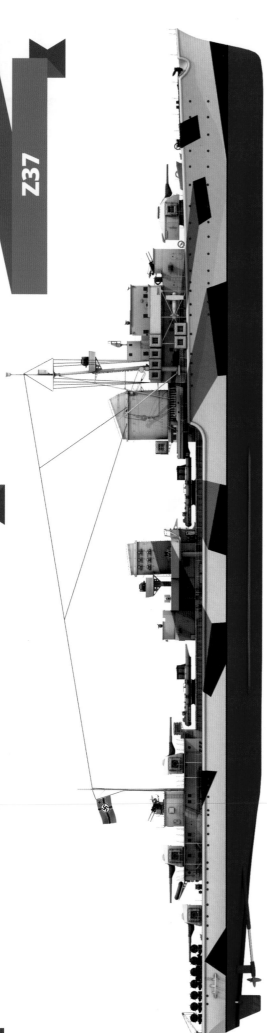

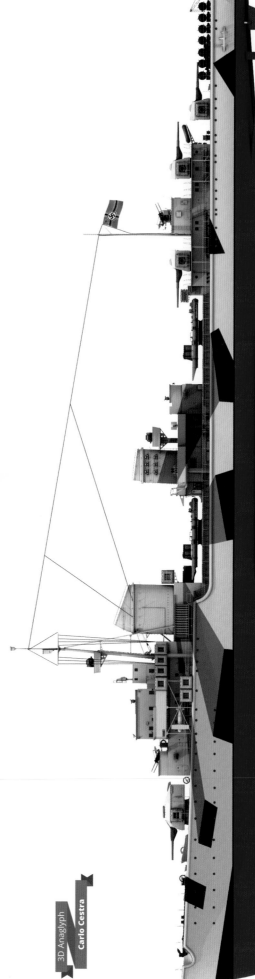

3D Anaglyph

Carlo Cestra

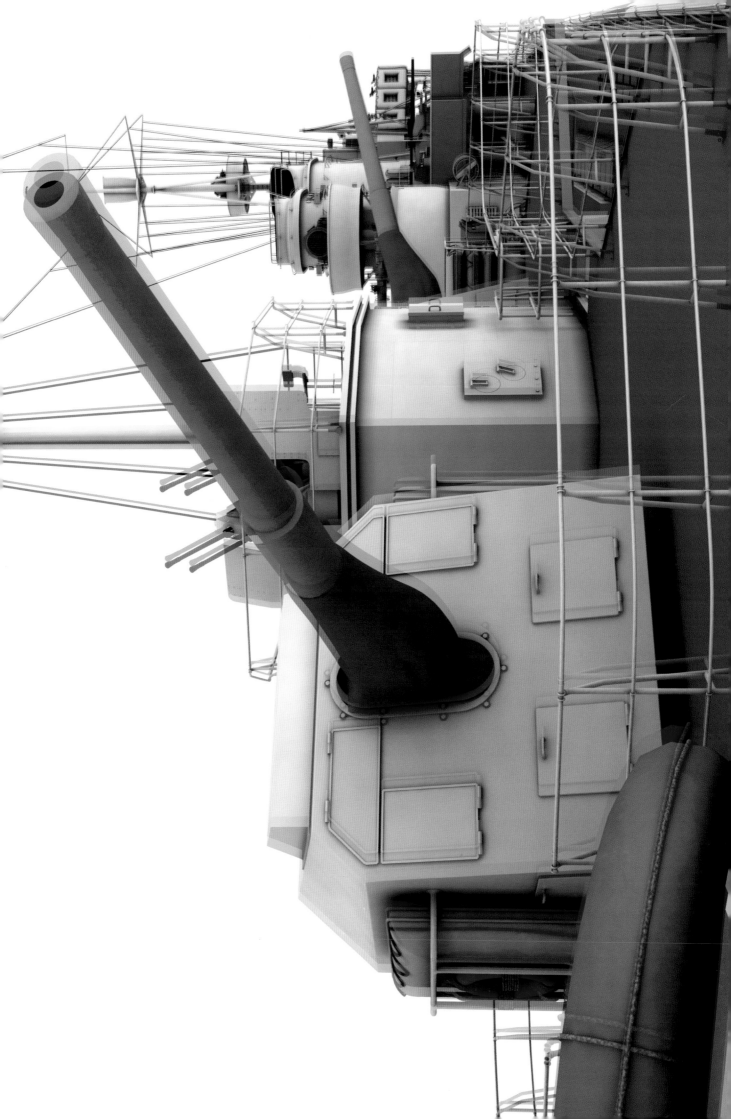